Healing with Kiryo

The Adventures and Teachings of Tadashi Kanzawa

This is an English translation of the original Japanese version published in 2004:

KIRYO DE KENKO ZOSHIN by Tadashi Kanzawa

(『気療で健康増進』神沢 瑞至 著)

Translation by Nimish Pratha

Assisting Translators: Aska Kuwabara, and Keith Murray Lewandowski

Editing and Revisions: Melissa Bell, James Van Gelder

First published in USA by Wheel of Knowledge Publishing in 2018

ISBN-13: 978-0996192934 ISBN-10: 099619293X

Wheel of Knowledge Publications

www.WheelofKnowledge.org

Introduction

I have a saying: "Ki is existence itself." And just as this saying predicts, through Kiryo (treatment), many people have healed their illnesses and injuries and restored the health of their natural existences. And that is not all. As I saw these people gain the ability to perceive Ki as they recovered, I deepened my belief that "Ki is possessed by all."

The two works that precede this (*Kiryo* and *Remote Kiryo*) were centered around treatment and implementation; that focus remains in this book as well. The many Kiryo practitioners around the world have put this focus into practice to great effect. Kiryo possesses marvelous healing power, and it may be said that as long as its results remain spectacular, one need not debate about its theoretical basis.

However, as I consider the matter now, even if we attempt to theoretically debate the particulars of Kiryo, there is a near-complete lack of vocabulary and phraseology to describe it. Thus, discussion has been simply limited to a listing of the achievements of Kiryo.

In 1996, I opened the Kiryo Academy. Initially, however, I struggled to instruct my students as I lacked both the theory and terminology to explain Kiryo. One day, the Kiryo recipients and students at the academy began to express their sensations upon receiving Ki as "tingling" or "cool, blowing" feelings. Through the various words they used, I realized that these students may actually be expressing the true nature of Ki itself. I theorized that in their expressions, they were articulating the activity of their sensory nerves—that is, their perceptive and differentiative abilities—upon being exposed to Kiryo.

I then struggled to name the sensory nerves that perceive and discriminate Ki energy. I decided that Ki energy would be the domain of the "Kiryo nerves" and the power of perceiving and discrimination would be the function of the "Wave Sensory Nerves." The details of these are explained in Chapter 2 of this book, "Discovery of the Two Sensory Nerves". These concepts are not recognized in modern medicine and are part of the unique point of view of Kiryo.

Since discovering the two sensory nerves and verbalizing their sensory phenomena, words such as "collective energy" and "peaceful space" have been coined, and the educated of Academy students has become much easier. The numbers of practitioners and students has risen, and the Academy is brimming with vigor.

Now, some ten years later, I have decided to author this book with two motivations in mind.

The first is that I had come to realize that Kiryo is not just treatment. Through its mastery exercises, one is able to master the following four things: ① Ki energy; ② ability of perception and discrimination; ③ preventative Kiryo (preventing illness before it occurs); and ④ worsening prevention (halting the worsening of illnesses and restoring one's health). All of these things are explained in great detail in this book, and I invite you to review them herein.

The second is that in 2002, the "Health Promotion Act" was promulgated. Given the aging of Japanese society and its low birthrate, and the need to address lifestyle diseases and the like, this law aims to urge each Japanese citizen to manage their own health and strive to promote it.

I think that the mastery of Kiryo and the aim of the Health Promotion Act are one and the same. I hope that at least one person will read this book, commit themselves to Kiryo mastery (exercise), and thereby recover and promote their health.

Lastly, in compiling this book, I am glad to have had the encouragement and assistance of Ryoji Takabayashi, a Kiryo practitioner and an editorial department official at my publishing company. I express my sincere gratitude for his help.

Tadashi Kanzawa

New Year 2004

Table of Contents

Chapter 1: Ki Exchange with Animals

How I Came to Be on TV

It was a cold, gray, and cloudy day in the middle of February 2001. At the invitation of a friend, I went to a zoo and walked around looking at the various animals. Stopping in front of the gorilla enclosure, I felt the sudden urge to transmit Ki. This was because I remembered what I had done on TV. On TBS TV's "Bizarre Animals", I put the "Apologizing Monkey[1]" to sleep, and on Fuji TV's "Miracle Experiences! Unbelievable!" I made a raccoon relax.

However, we were outside and there were other people watching. I'd never done something quite like this, and I thought this might just be impossible. Two of the gorillas playing in the enclosure were rather far from me, so I began to transmit Ki to the gorilla which was a bit closer. The distance was about ten meters.

Four to five minutes passed, and then suddenly the gorilla began scratching itself all over its body. The feedback sensation in the palm of the hand I was using to transmit Ki strengthened, and I felt like I'd begun exchanging Ki with the gorilla. After three to four minutes, the gorilla went and hid behind a large rock

---

[1] A trained monkey that was quite popular on Japanese TV in the 90s.

in its enclosure. Luckily, from where I was standing, its chest and head were still visible. After about a minute or two, the gorilla yawned several times and fell asleep.

My friend, who had watched this entire process unfold from beginning to end, was quite surprised. I was, too. It was undeniable that the gorilla had been put to sleep by the Ki energy that I transmitted to it. It was proof of the power of Ki.

After this, I interacted with various animals; this, however, was the incident that marked the beginning of my efforts to further confirm the existence of Ki.

One day, the friend that had witnessed my interaction with the gorilla at the zoo asked if I would like to appear on an Asahi TV program. I did not know what the content of the program would be, so we decided to meet again.

In early March, four representatives from Asahi TV came to my apartment. They told me the station was trying to start a new program in April called "Strange Sudden TV. Is that Real?" (Saturday evenings, 7:00pm-8:00pm), and they wanted to ask me to participate. The basic concept of the show was that it would showcase strange, miraculous things and occurrences from around the world.

For the first episode, they wanted to document the effects of Ki energy on animals: what sort of state it puts them in, whether they sleep or relax, how they lay down, etc. The first animal they had in mind to demonstrate this was an elephant. I was surprised by this. I had always wanted to make an animal as large as an elephant lay down. It had been a dream of mine for quite a while, but never did I even think I'd get a chance to actually try. However, truth be told, I was actually quite worried about whether or not an animal the size of an elephant would be swayed at all by my efforts.

When I voiced this feeling to the staff members, they told me that they didn't mind if I failed, and that I should just give it a go. So, I accepted their offer.

Ki Exchange with Animals

Having received my consent, Asahi TV set up the shoot in a zoo. They brought in a Thai elephant. The personnel present were myself, the director, the assistant director, the cameraman, and his assistants. The zoo had also arranged for some employees to be there: their Japanese chief zookeeper, a Thai zookeeper, and some others. In total, there were about ten people.

By 3:00 PM, the rain that'd been falling since morning stopped, preparations were finally complete, and we were told to be on standby.

Finally, filming began. I concealed my fears about whether or not the elephant would actually lay down and went to stand in the place where I was told that I'd be transmitting Ki.

From inside a small trainer's enclosure came an elephant with a Thai zookeeper on its back. About ten meters away from where I stood, the zookeeper dismounted the elephant. As it stood there, I began transmitting Ki.

The waves of the elephant flowed into my palm. My feedback sensation (explained later) grew stronger and stronger. The elephant drew closer to me at a leisurely pace. It was now three meters between myself and the elephant. I didn't move a muscle. I felt neither awe nor fear.

After about five minutes, the elephant began to sway side-to-side while slowly retreating backwards. Suddenly, the elephant fell over with a loud crash. As soon as the elephant began to sway, the Thai handler yelled out something. It hadn't even been ten minutes since I'd started transmitting Ki. Nevertheless, the elephant had already laid down. Given the short amount of time, I immediately thought that this was all arranged beforehand. I thought the Thai zookeeper had directed the elephant to lie down.

I felt myself becoming angry. From behind me, the director remarked, "Well done Professor, you succeeded!" but in my anger I was making a disgruntled face.

We got the elephant back up, and I began to transmit Ki again. After about five minutes, the large body of the elephant began to sway deeply from side-to-side, and it collapsed once more with a resounding crash. Once again, the Thai zookeeper yelled out something just before. We again got up the stretched-out elephant, and I began transmitting Ki for the third time. Almost immediately, the large body of the elephant again began to sway deeply.

This time, it made a great trumpeting noise before falling, and it seemed its right hindleg buckled beneath it. Not 30 minutes had passed since filming began.

Given how little time had passed, and how many times I was able to make the elephant fall, I was still convinced that this had all been faked. Almost immediately after the end of filming was announced, I asked the chief zookeeper whether the Thai zookeeper had instructed the elephant to fall. He assured me no such thing had happened, and that the Thai words the zookeeper had used meant, "The elephant's going to fall! Watch out!" I was still unconvinced, so I asked him if he was surprised that the elephant fell. He immediately said, "No, no," and gave me the following explanation.

There are two times an elephant will lay on its side. The first is when, having confirmed that there are no threats around it, it lays on its side to frolic and play. The second one is when its skin is itchy, but there are no trees around to scratch it against it, so it lays down to rub its sides against the ground to relieve the itching. In fact, there was something else that was quite surprising.

This was the fact that, despite being surrounded by a number of people's voices conversing, the elephant had closed its ears and eyes, and was standing with the knee of its left foreleg tilted away from the ground. In particular, the chief zookeeper was surprised that it had closed its ears, as this meant that it was in a complete state of relaxation, and was sleeping.

I realized something as I listened to the chief zookeeper's explanation. The elephant had fallen down because it itchy.

This fit with what I knew from Kiryo theory. When one receives Ki energy, muscular adjustment and blood flow promotion occurs inside the body. In the case of this elephant, just like the gorilla mentioned before, when it received Ki from me, muscle adjustment occurred, its blood flow improved, and its skin became itchy. Unable to bear this, it laid down.

Reflecting on what they'd learned about the greatness of Ki, I exchanged handshakes with all the people present. Unfortunately, only a short clip of the elephant falling down made it to the broadcast.

Australia (Aired Saturday, April 14, 2001)

A few days later, I was contacted again by Asahi TV, and they asked me if I would go to Australia for them. Apparently, a competition called a "rodeo," where people compete to see how long they can ride on a wild bull's back, had been held the other day in Australia. The current record was three seconds. In the competition that had just happened, a young competitor had been thrown from the back of the bull, which then picked him up with its horns and threw him more than ten meters, injuring his ribs in the process.

Apparently, this young man wanted to compete again, and hoped I could use Kiryo to make the bull more compliant. Asahi TV wanted to get footage of the young man breaking the record and setting a new one. Upon hearing this I thought something to myself. Usually, when receiving Ki, animals get more energetic, so I wondered what would happen.

In any case, I had never done any of this outside, much less abroad, so I realized that there'd be no way to know for sure without giving it a try. I took them up on their offer.

Thus, on March 13th, 2001, I departed Narita Airport for Australia with the Asahi TV staff.

After arriving at Melbourne Airport, we left for the location. Along the way, we stopped at a zoo, and scenes of me transmitting Ki to the animals there were shot. I transmitted Ki to the animal emblematic of Australia itself: the kangaroo. One kangaroo laid down in less than two minutes. Soon after, the second laid down, and when I turned around to look at the rest, all 30 were on the ground. I was surprised. It took scarcely 10 minutes for this to happen. I tried this with koalas as well, but as they don't move much, it didn't really have the same visual effect.

#Picture 1: Soon after, these kangaroos had all laid down.

#Picture1: Viking and the author.

#Picture2: Viking was released into the barred enclosure behind me.

I also transmitted Ki to a giant tortoise, which then drew up against the fence between us and blew its nose. That was funny! Apparently, its stuffed nose had cleared up. Eventually, we arrived at our intended destination, which was in a field. My showdown with these wild bulls drew nearer and nearer.

Not soon after we had arrived, six wild bulls were released into a barred enclosure that had been set up in this field. My task was to dominate the strongest of these bulls, Viking, and make him more compliant. The young rider would then get up onto his back and try to hang on for more than three seconds, and thereby set a new record.

I began to transmit Ki to the six bulls in the enclosure. I was slightly worried that they might not actually fall over. About ten minutes passed without incident. Then one bull's hips began to shake. Suddenly, the forelegs of the animal gave way, its hips dropped, and it fell on its side. Only its head stayed up.

I exclaimed to myself, "I did it!" I decided I would try to use "Sole of the Foot Kiryo" (explained later) to dominate the remaining animals, so the staff prepared a chair for me.

They placed the chair about three meters away from the enclosure. I sat myself down on it, raised my right leg up, turned the sole of my foot towards the bulls, and began to transmit Ki. Soon, the forelegs of the remaining bulls gave way, and they crumpled to the ground.

The sight these of five bulls keeling over while keeping their heads aloft was quite striking. Now there was just one bull left— Viking himself. I stood up from my chair and began to transmit Ki to Viking, again using the palm of my right hand.

He refused to give in. He would totter about, and sometimes look as if he was about to fall, but at the last moment, he would dig his heels in and stay standing. I could distinctly feel his strong energy radiating through the air. I realized that I would have to rely on my last resort. All people present, myself included, distanced themselves from Viking in an effort to prevent him from noticing our human auras. I decided I would try to use remote Kiryo on Viking, which is when someone transmits Ki over a large distance.

The first step of remote Kiryo is to confirm the Ki exchange; I did so, using my right hand to check the exchange between myself and Viking. In a sense, this process can be thought of as "catching" the waves of information being sent out by Viking's body. Then, I distanced myself from him, all the while checking the integrity of the exchange between us using the palm of my hand.

Strangely, the more that I distanced myself, the stronger the hand feedback sensation in my palm grew. I approached and stood upon an embankment about 50 meters away from Viking. From the top of this embankment, I turned my right palm to Viking and waved it up and down, continuing to transmit Ki the whole time.

After about five minutes, I felt a powerful recoil in my hand. Something had changed inside Viking. Knowing that he would fall, I cried out, "He's going down!" At that moment, Viking's forelegs gave way, his knees buckled, and he crumbled to the ground. Before I knew it, I'd cried out, "I did it!"

Viking had reached a state of relaxation.

Finally, the time had come. Preparations in the arena had been completed. Even a local TV station was on the scene.

The young man attempting this challenge again came and shook my hand. We were told to be on standby, and Viking was brought into the small pen where one gets on the bull's back in a rodeo. He was raging violently. I decided to transmit Ki to Viking through the steel fencing panels. Viking still lashing out, spearing the steel fencing panels with his horns and throwing his whole weight at them. I simply continued to transmit Ki to him.

As I was standing quite close to the fencing panels, I could feel the full intensity of his anger. Strangely, I was not scared. The young man was watching Viking, trying to figure out the best time to mount him. I drew away from Viking, exited the fenced enclosure, and continued to transmit Ki. The moment the young man jumped onto Viking's violently thrashing back, the gate to the small pen was thrown open. Hang on for more than three seconds, I thought. However, the moment Viking exited his small pen, the body of the young man, thrown upwards by Viking's spasms, flew through the air and hit the dirt.

The young man's riding time was 1.96 seconds. He had failed his challenge. He was very disappointed. I was, too.

However, the fact that we were able to confirm the existence of a Ki exchange sensation in animals was a huge development for Kiryo.

Spain (Aired 2001 October 13, broadcast)

This time, the schedule was a little bit tight. On September 15, 2001 at 1pm, I departed Narita for De Gaulle. I arrived at my hotel near the Arc de Triomphe in Paris on the evening of the 15th, local time. The next day, I gave lectures, lead exercises, and did demonstrations of Kiryo (treatment) at the Paris branch of the Academy. The following day, the 17th, I held classes focused on Kiryo mastery (exercise).

Then, on the morning of the 18th, I left a north Paris train station for Wuppertal, Germany, on the TGV bullet train.

At eight o'clock on the night of the 19th, I departed Dusseldorf for Spain. Asahi TV staff greeted me at the airport in Madrid, the capital.

Finally, on the next day, the 20th, the shoot commenced. I departed the hotel in which I was staying at 8 AM and headed for a sheep farm. When I arrived at the farm, I saw what were to be the subjects for this experiment: three hundred sheep. Though they were sheep, their movements were rather powerful and vigorous, and I wondered to myself whether or not this would all turn out okay. However, because I'd already had my successes with the elephant and the kangaroos, I had some confidence.

Despite the fact that only the collapse of two of the kangaroos was shown on the program, I'd actually put three to sleep, and, upon turning around, found that more than 30 of them had fallen down behind me. They fell down due to a Ki response chain.

I faced the 300-odd sheep that had been gathered together using the slope of a small hill near us and began transmitting Ki. This was the first time I had ever transmitted Ki to so many animals.

Although I began transmitting Ki in a slightly excited state, I strangely began to calm down as I continued.

After about five minutes had passed, I noticed a change in the state of the sheep. The sheep's heads had begun to droop somewhat, and in places several of them were snuggling together. Small groups (clumps) of sheep had formed, and the movements of even the sheep around them were growing slower.

At this time, there were a few people that were speaking loudly and moving around, so the sheep began to raise their heads again.

I quickly told them in a stern voice to "be quiet!" This was because I remembered what had happened on a program I had appeared in, Fuji TV's "Miraculous Experiences! Unbelievable!"

The object of the program was to capture footage of me putting a raccoon to sleep. Beforehand, the raccoon and its handler entered my dressing room at the Fuji TV studio where the shoot was to take place. There was still a bit of time before the shoot was scheduled to begin, so I was chatting with the handler, but I suddenly felt a desire to try to transmit Ki to the raccoon. There were about 5 meters between us. The raccoon had been running about in its cage, but it soon became quiet and still. I continued to send Ki to it, and as I drew closer to its cage, the animal laid down and suddenly fell asleep. I was quite surprised by how quickly all this happened.

The handler reached inside the cage, picked up the sleeping raccoon, and petted its body and face. It still did not wake, so he put his finger in its ear. I also tried pulling gently on its leg. It remained asleep. I remarked in jest, "I'm counting on this for the real shoot, too," as the raccoon slept. Soon after, I entered the studio, and filming started.

Counting the hundred or so spectators, the emcee, the special guests, the cameramen, and various other staff, there were a few hundred people inside the studio. People were talking, the lights were bright, and several machines were humming along. The entire room was bustling. Amidst all this, the rather excited raccoon made its entrance. I began to transmit Ki to it as it remained in its cage. After about five minutes, the raccoon had calmed down considerably. Two or three minutes later, it had laid down, but it had not yet fallen asleep. And despite the fact that it had fallen asleep so beautifully in my dressing room, when it was in the studio, it was stressed and on alert, and though I could get it to relax, it was impossible to put it to sleep.

Because of this experience, I realized how important it was to make sure to not stress or alert the sheep. I instructed everyone on the scene to be quiet.

Again, I began to transmit Ki, and after about five minutes, one sheep lowered its head, bent its forelegs, and laid down. They began to fall in twos and threes, and the sheep around them in the small groups they'd formed also began to lay down. It was a rather interesting sight. And as I turned towards the ones that remained, and sent Ki towards them, I felt a strong, forceful feedback sensation, and the sheep fell. The bodily information of these sheep was streaming into me through my hand.

The announcer that had been commentating the proceedings exclaimed in a surprised voice, "Look! It's like a carpet of sheep!" And indeed, looking out, more than eighty sheep had already laid down. I was surprised myself. I then suggested to the announcer that we should try aiming for individual sheep. I would point my finger in a direction, the staff would confirm it, and then, upon sending Ki in that direction, the sheep there would fall down, asleep. They were falling left and right.

Picture1#: Flock of sheep and the author (second from the right), performing Kiryo.

Picture 2#: The sheep fell one after another.

The announcer had a face of complete disbelief. Just thirty minutes had passed since I had begun transmitting Ki, and yet one could look out and see over a hundred sheep stretched out on the ground like a massive carpet. It was difficult for us to count an exact number from where we were standing on the slope, but it appeared that most of the sheep had toppled over. The sheep that were still standing were not moving a muscle. They were comfortably paralyzed. It was almost as if time itself had stopped. We were in a silent, unspeakably healing Ki space.

The owner of the farm also had a disbelieving expression on his face, and his mouth was hanging open. It would be no exaggeration to say that everyone present, myself included, was in a world beyond their wildest imaginations. Soon after, the staff all left the farm in a tizzy.

On the 21st, the next day, at about 8 in the morning, I left my hotel for a satellite city of Madrid called San Sebastian; my destination was its bull fighting arena. This particular shoot had required a huge amount of planning and preparation, and I realized it would be unforgivable if I were to fail here.

The set consisted of a metal cage that I would stand inside, a steel fence, a camera crane, and the usual cameras. Three bullfighters that had agreed to appear in the program were standing by, as were various emergency personnel: an ambulance, a doctor, and a nurse. City ordinances dictated that certain medical professionals must be present whenever a bullfight takes place.

The author and the matadors (bullfighters).

The setup inside the bullfighting arena and the camera crane.

The showdown was now just minutes away. To show just how ferocious this bull was, a "Kanzawa doll" was made to wear red clothing and was placed in the center of the arena. The gate opened and the bull, Bogabante, was allowed into the arena. The moment it laid eyes on the Kanzawa doll, it charged forward furiously. In flash, the Kanzawa doll met a pitiful end, cruelly ripped to pieces. I was overcome by the fearsome intensity of the spectacle, and I began to worry.

Next, three matadors (bullfighters) appeared. They put on a powerful show as Bogabante chased them around the arena. It was now my turn to appear, and after taking a few "cool" shots alongside the matadors, my showdown began.

I entered the steel-barred cage set up in the arena and patiently waited for Bogabante to come. I wasn't scared in the slightest. The gate opened. Bogabante made a majestic entrance into the arena. He stopped near the middle of the arena and looked this way and that, taking in his surroundings. He noticed me behind the steel bars and drew closer . As I continued to transmit Ki to him, Bogabante squared off with me, and charged the cage with his horns as if he was trying to toss it into the air. He rammed his horns into its steel bars five times.

He caught sight of the black cloth covering the steel fence set in front of my cage, and started ferociously thrusting his horns against it. Entangled in his horns, his fierce vigor tore it to shreds. He turned again towards me, and in his rage tried to uproot and destroy the steel bars between us so he could attack me. Without any fear, I simply allowed myself to be a medium for natural energy and send Ki to the rampaging Bogabante.

After about ten minutes, Bogabante had calmed down somewhat. I decided to perform body feedback exchange. I crossed my legs, placed my awareness throughout my body, and used it to transmit Ki. As I continued transmitting Ki from this position, Bogabante slowly began to relax and his rage abated.

Then, I exited the steel cage, walked around behind it, and stood in the upper levels of the bleachers, from where I began to transmit Ki to Bogabante using remote Kiryo. However, whenever anyone moved, Bogabante would immediately react. It didn't seem like he was going to fall asleep at all. Remembering what had happened with the sheep the previous day, I decided to make use of the chain reaction. I also realized that Bogabante's alerted state would be calmed if he had a few bovine friends with him. We asked the owner of the area if he had any more cows. He told us he had three beef cattle and allowed us to borrow them.

The three cattle were released into the arena. From the bleachers, I again began to transmit Ki to the four bulls. There were about forty meters between us. And perhaps because he had relaxed a bit due to the arrival of his friends, Bogabante, who had been violently rampaging until a few minutes ago, started to yawn. One of the beef cattle folded the knees of its front legs and laid down.

But Bogabante would not follow suit. So I took a gamble. I proposed to the owner and the staff that I would stand at the protective fence used by the bullfighters near the arena and wave my hands and a towel. If Bogabante charged me, I would lose, but if he didn't, I would win. They agreed, and everyone except the owner ascended to the upper levels of the stands.

I began my final showdown. From behind the defensive barrier, I faced Bogabante and waved first one, and then both hands. Next, I provoked Bogabante with a towel. And rather than charge me, Bogabante actually retreated. The power of Ki had completely erased his warlike instincts as a fighting bull. The owner of the bullring, who had watched all this unfold, told us he'd never seen a fighting bull yawn in the arena or retreat when provoked with a towel. "This must be a miracle!" he exclaimed.

In this way, my showdown with a fighting bull ended in victory for me. It was a magnificent proof of the Ki energy "chain reaction."

Kenya, Africa (Aired December 22, 2001)

On November 27th, 2001, at 6:10 AM, I arrived at Nairobi airport. The air in Kenya was brilliant and clear, and it was neither too hot nor cold.

Despite having just been on planes for about 20 hours, I wasn't particularly exhausted. In the parking lot of the airport, some Asahi TV staff had already begun preparing for the shoot. I changed into my usual robes, and we began the six-hour journey to the Maasai village that would be the setting for this program. Upon leaving Nairobi, we entered the vast savannah. I noticed how wonderfully gently the grass on these plains waved in the wind; it was a profoundly soothing sight.

Though they were at an altitude of 1,500 meters above sea level, these savannahs were the perfect habitat for countless different animals. As we passed through these plains, where the sky and earth meet, I could feel with my very body the grandeur of nature. I recalled a manga with which I was enthralled in my youth called "Young Kenya," and I realized that my long-held dream of coming to the wilds of Africa had finally become reality. However, the rough car ride took its toll, and the five-day shoot was tough.

Finally, the time came for me to begin Ki exchange with the animals. Whenever I stand in front of animals with the aim of performing Ki exchange with them, I always wonder if they'll actually fall down or not. After all, as always, this was a new experience. But my inner self knew that if I did not give it a try, I'd never know the result.

However, as I began the showdown and Ki exchange was started, all my wonderings and misgivings were swept away, my mind cleared, and I entered a state of nothingness. It really is quite strange how that happens. I allow myself to become a medium for the natural energy known as Ki, and I cannot but help feeling and being as I am. As I was in Kenya, I was able to meld myself with the vastness of the savannah and unify myself with the energies of the animals in front of me.

The Kenyan animals in front of me received my Ki energy, muscular adjustment began, their blood flow improved, they entered a state of relaxation, became comfortable, and finally grew sleepy. Their feelings of alarm and unease fade away, as do their fight-or-flight instincts, and they cannot help but collapse.

Below, I will discuss in order the scenes and hand feedback sensations (the animals' waves) that resulted from the series of Ki exchanges I performed.

Before that, I would like to draw your attention to the fact that there is a definite pattern that typifies Ki exchange from beginning to end. While this does vary somewhat on the animal being interacted with, in general, I begin transmitting Ki, and after about five minutes, I experience a change in my hand feedback.

Kangaroos and rhinoceroses fall down with a thud, fast asleep, in as little as three minutes after beginning to transmit Ki, but for other animals, it takes a bit longer, and they fall asleep slower. It takes about five minutes for the hand feedback sensation to become stronger.

This hand feedback sensation takes the form of a feeling of pain or a feeling that is like pain. It is different for different people, but the sensation generally varies along three dimensions: its strength or weakness; its type (electric tingling, etc.), and its hardness or softness (or tightness vs. looseness). In particular, the type of the sensation, and how it is described will vary considerably from person to person. For example, it can occur as throbbing, twitching, tingling, or burning, or as a feeling of compression, heat, or weight.

By noticing changes in these sensations, one can catch with the palm of the hand information about the changes occurring inside the receiving animal's body—bodily information—as waves. This is something anyone can learn to do with just a bit of practice. In about 30 minutes, one can create a Ki energy space, a healing space, and the animals inside it will lay down, relax, and even fall asleep.

I will now discuss the various Ki exchanges with animals, the scenes, and hand feedback sensations in the order that these episodes were aired by Asahi TV. But first, let me talk about the environment I experienced in Kenya.

It was the end of November, but the skies were often clear, and the sunlight was rather strong. Strong enough for my face to get rather tanned. It didn't rain at all, and during the day, the temperature was about 86 degrees, but, as humidity was low, it didn't feel very hot. However, temperatures fell at night, and in the early morning, it was often in the low 40s, so one had to use a   hot   water   bottle   to   stay   warm. I stayed in a tent made of a thick fabric inside which a bed, toilet, shower, table, and other amenities had been placed.

We were staying in the savannahs of the great African plains; the area was dotted with small copses[2] of trees and the only road was a one-lane dirt track. To find the animals we needed for our shoots, I would spend two to three hours in the back of a jeep as it traversed the roadless plains, my body jostled about by the rough terrain. The days were long and hard, but the winds of the great plains were gentle. These were the circumstances that surrounded my showdowns with the animals of Africa.

---

[2] A small group of trees.

The first animal was a topi.

The topi are called the lookouts of savanna: nervous and alert, eyes wary and watching. They look much like hornless deer. After beginning to transmit Ki to a group of twenty topi about twenty meters away from us, it took some time for them to fall down. I guess they really are very vigilant.

The feedback sensation I felt from them was soft and crackly. It took about 15 minutes for them to stop moving and begin to lower their heads. One of the twenty-odd animals began scrabbling at the ground with his forelegs, which suddenly bent, sending him to the ground. The twitching feeling in my palm grew stronger.

One after another, the topi before me pawed the ground and then fell.

After 30 minutes the healing space was complete and most of the topi had fallen down. Then, from far off, several zebras approached, passing right in front of me as they entered the healing space. They began rubbing their bodies against nearby trees as they entered a state of relaxation.

As my showdown was now over, the driver brought the car once around the group of topi. Although some did stand, not a single one attempted to run away. Within the group there was also a fox-like gazelle that was lying on its side, fast asleep. All of them were completely relaxed.

The local area coordinator who saw this was so moved that he declared he'd changed his outlook on life. Before I'd started transmitting Ki to the topi he'd assured me that "topi are always alert and vigilant. There's no way they'll fall." It must have been hard for him to believe his eyes as those same topi fell down one after another in comfortable bliss.

My next encounter was with zebras.

As our car sprinted across the great plains, we saw in the distance a group of about thirty zebras. I positioned myself about thirty meters away from them and began to transmit Ki. Five minutes later, the hand feedback sensation in my palm began to grow stronger. Twenty more minutes passed. The zebra had grown still.

Suddenly, two fell down, stuck their four legs up in the sky, and began to rub their backs against the ground. They were playing in the sand. Having been sent Ki, their blood flow had improved, making their bodies itchy. As there were no trees around, they had no choice but to fall down and rub their backs on the ground.

My third encounter was with lions.

Traveling across the great plains, we encountered a male lion. Recognizing the danger, I put about forty meters between him and myself and began to transmit Ki. This was the animal I had most wanted to meet while in Africa. After two to three minutes of transmitting, the male lion stretched out his front legs and promptly fell asleep. It was all over so fast that it felt a bit unsatisfying.

Not soon after, in another area, we came across a family of two parents and two cubs. All four of them yawned quickly went into state of relaxation and laid down on their sides. Because lions sleep through most of the day, the Maasai people that witnessed this remained unconvinced that Ki had put these animals to sleep.

The fourth encounter was with cheetahs.

As we raced across the great plains, we found a family of four cheetahs. The moment I began transmitting Ki, the male and female began to move apart. The male then began chasing after the female and their cubs.

As the cheetahs appeared to be in such a good mood, I was able to transmit Ki just ten meters from them. Within fifteen minutes, they had started yawning, and they soon laid on their side and fell asleep. There were two other cars that had accompanied us, and with our three, there were five in total. All five drove towards and encircled the cheetahs. Yet, even though they were with their cubs, none of the cheetahs showed signs of alarm, and they remained completely relaxed. Unfortunately, the Maasai people refused once again to recognize this event as having been brought about by Ki energy.

My fifth encounter was with a hippopotamus.

I stood on the banks of the murky river Mara, which runs through the Maasai village, and began to transmit Ki into its unfathomable depths. Apparently, there were hippopotamuses in the river. The feedback sensation in the palm of my hand grew stronger.

Before I realized it, hippopotamuses from both upstream and downstream were drawing together and approaching me. I was surprised. The employees of a nearby hotel were also quite surprised; this was the first time they'd seen so many hippopotamuses collecting together in one place. Hippopotamuses are very territorial, so they do not normally group together in this manner.

Then, two of the ten-odd hippopotamuses present fell asleep, and although hippopotamus do not fall asleep in the water, before long it had closed its eyes and sunk into the water. Seeing this, the hotel employees were astonished beyond words.

My sixth encounter was with a giraffe.

As we were racing across the great plains one day, we spotted a copse of trees, with four giraffes near them. One of the things I was most looking forward to seeing was a giraffe falling over. We had hoped to make the children that would watch this TV show happy by showing a giraffe fall over but the one in front of us wasn't being very cooperative. It simply would not fall down. What a shame. A complete failure. Thinking back, I get the feeling that the feedback sensation in the palm of my hand was weak, as was the feedback in the soles of my feet.

My seventh encounter was with a rhinoceros.

We entered a forest known to contain rhinoceroses, and after traveling for a bit, we encountered one. According to the Maasai people, it was on its way to the river to drink.

I immediately moved to a spot about ten meters away from it and began to transmit Ki. The moment the Ki exchange began, I felt a powerful feedback sensation in my right hand (the one I was using to send Ki). My hand clenched up into a fist, and creaking pain raced across the back of it. Continuing to transmit Ki, I drew nearer to the animal, stopping about five meters away from it.

Once two or three minutes had passed since I began transmitting Ki, the rhinoceros, which had stopped moving earlier, began to walk again, headed for the shade of a nearby tree. It plopped down its more than four tons of body weight with a resounding crash, and after raising its head and snorting once, it fell deeply asleep. I was just three meters away from it. Barely three minutes had passed. The Maasai people that witnessed this were beside themselves with amazement.

This was the first time I had experienced such fierce pain in the palm of my hand during Ki exchange. Just like the rhinoceros that caused it, it was simply gargantuan.

A rhino on its way to the river. Afterwards, upon receiving my Ki, it went under the shade of a nearby tree and fell down with a crash.

My eighth encounter was with an elephant.

Racing our car across the great plains, we came across a herd of elephants. There were more than 300 of them. They'd broken of into smaller groups that were scattered about close to each other. I selected a group that had about fifty and began to transmit Ki to it.

The elephants were leisurely eating and walking. Almost immediately after I'd begun to transmit Ki, they stopped their movement and drew closer to our vehicle. From above the open roof of our vehicle, they reached out with their trunks to me. The Maasai people cried out, "Be careful of those trunks! They can throw you!" Strangely, I felt no fear. But the presence of these majestic animals was incredibly electrifying.

After I'd been transmitting Ki for about fifteen minutes, the elephants laid themselves down near a watering hole. They started played in the mud, rubbing it all over themselves. One of them laid down on top of a thicket and did not raise itself for some time.

The Maasai people had cocked their heads to one side, and had quizzical expressions on their faces. It seemed that they didn't want to acknowledge the power of Ki. However, I knew that my Ki had caused muscular adjustment in the elephants, increasing their blood flow, and, due to the lack of trees on the great plains, they'd fallen down to scratch themselves against the ground. I had also felt a rather significant hand feedback sensation when exchanging with them.

The ninth encounter was with buffalo.

Before going to try and make the buffalo fall asleep, I visited an elder of the Maasai village. The houses of their village were arranged in a circular shape with a circular plaza in the middle. There were about forty houses total. The houses were built simply; the walls were made of cow dung. As I walked into the middle of the plaza, the ground beneath my leather sandals squelched. It, too, was made of cow dung. Cow dung is immensely important to the Maasai people. It is used to make fire and to drive away insects; it is an indispensable item for everyday life.

I went to the place of the elder and greeted him with the customary "Jambo!" I remember well the sharp glint in his eye, and his piercing gaze. I told him that I wanted to use the power of Ki to make animals fall down. "Such a thing is impossible," the elder replied. I showed him the video we had of me defeating a topi, and the elder made a disbelieving face. He then asked whether I would attempt to do the same with the water buffalo, an animal far more dangerous than even the lion. The emcee of the program asked, "What d'ya think, Mr. Kanzawa?"

"Let's do it," I replied. Some of the Maasai people were selected to bear witness to our agreement. The emcee, myself, and the Maasai witnesses all shook hands firmly.

The author participating in a Maasai dance

29

Not long after, Maasai men and women of all ages had gathered together in a large group outside. The young people then began to dance, chanting "Ehho! Ehho!" Suddenly, the elder grabbed my hand and pulled me into the middle of their circle. I had absolutely no idea what I was doing, but I tried my best to chant "Ehho!" and dance in sync with them. Watching me, the staff present began to laugh and sway with the beat of the dance.

After some time, the dancing stopped, and the jumping began. They insisted that I jump with them. Without any way to refuse, I joined them, and was met with another chorus of laughter.

Eventually, even the announcer, in his business suit, was made to jump. I later learned that that dance is an ancient one, passed down from generation to generation, and only performed to stir up the courage of a young Maasai boy before his rite of passage into manhood: the lion hunt. All the members of the tribe had danced for me, to stir up my own courage before my showdown with the water buffalo. I was deeply grateful.

Showdown with the Buffalo

My showdown (Ki exchange) with the water buffalo was one of the few truly unforgettable experiences of my life. We left our tents at six in the morning. It was a fairly cold one. For three hours, our cars raced across the great plains, my body feeling every bump and pothole of the roadless terrain. Suddenly, a herd buffalo materialized in the distance.

We approached them slowly, stopping the car about thirty meters away. While I was, at the time, rather confident about my chances with a cow, I truly had no idea what would happen with the two hundred buffalo before me. Yet I also knew, deep down, that I would never find out if I didn't try. Taking care to not disturb the buffalo, I stuck my body from the chest up out of the top of the car, aimed the palms of my hands towards them, and began to transmit Ki.

I felt a feedback sensation straight away. The herd, which had been milling around, gradually began to stop moving, and I could see, in places, several of the animals draw quite close to each other. Five minutes passed, and now most of the buffalo were not moving at all. I grew more convinced that I really would be able to make them fall. Though this wasn't the same sort of animal, I felt that things here would go just as they did with the bulls in Spain.

Not long after, one of the buffalo fell. Then another. And then the ones which had huddled together all fell at once. Buffalo were falling to the ground, their forelegs giving way left and right in a 180-degree arc all around. It was if someone had drawn a huge semicircle with me at the center. However, once about 70% had fallen, the driver of one of the cars accidentally pressed the horn, and the buffalo all instantly jumped to their feet again.

The staff told me we could end the showdown here, but, for some reason, I felt the need to confront them again. My competitive spirit was burning hotly. I stood on the roof of the car, and, though I know not why, I put my left hand on my waist, aimed my right hand towards the buffalo, and began waving it from left to right, tracing out the semicircular shape that they'd gathered into (refer to the photographs at the beginning of the book). The buffalo once again started to fall.

With each buffalo that fell, I felt a light thud in my palm. Every time I waved my hand in a big arc from left to right, buffalo would fall down, dozens at a time. I was quite surprised.

I continued to wave my hand back and forth. Very soon, of the near 200 that had been before me, only seven remained

31

standing. The power of Ki had been clearly and plainly demonstrated for all to see. The vast plain before me had been made into a Ki energy space, and, through a Ki chain reaction, every single buffalo—even the seven that remained standing—had slipped into a state of relaxation. For a few moments, they'd lost their alert wariness and their fight-or-flight instincts.

Because I'd become a medium for the natural energy known as Ki and sent it to the buffalo, my Ki and the Ki of the buffalo merged to form a collective energy. As a result, a vast relaxation (healing) space had been built on the great plains of Kenya.

Back to the Maasai Village

My showdown with the bulls had ended, and we visited the elder of the Maasai village with the news. Upon showing him the footage, he recognized the significance of our achievement, exclaiming, "This is amazing!" He then bestowed me with the title of Maasai shaman, "oloiboni," and a talisman made of woven gnu hair as proof of this status. Apparently, only great and special people are allowed to become oloiboni. I was thankful to receive these honors, and I shook hands with the elder before we parted ways.

Siberia (Aired October 12, 2001)

Showdown with a Brown Bear

On September 8th, 2001, at about 7:50pm, I departed Haneda Airport. After a layover at Aomori, I arrived at Khabarovsk Airport and stayed one night at a hotel there. The next day, I left Khabarovsk Airport for the provincial capital of Kamchatka, a city called Petropavlovsk-Kamchatsky. From there, I flew south by helicopter, finally landing at Kurile Lake, at the southernmost tip of the peninsula. The wind was strong, and for someone from Japan, the September weather was unbelievably cold.

On the 10th, heavy rain kept us on standby for the whole day.

The 11th was our last day at Kurile Lake, and the weather was absolutely terrible. Despite the raging storm and the extreme cold, we had no choice but to get the shoot done, so we dressed as warm and waterproof as we could and departed.

With a young ranger as our guide, we crossed Kurile Lake by motorboat, and arrived at a point on its shore that bears were known to appear. Sockeye salmon swam through the river there, and their carcasses, left half-eaten by bears, lay strewn about. From the edge of a cliff overlooking the river, I faced the forest on the other bank and began to transmit Ki into its depths. I continued to transmit for two hours, but we saw no sign that there were even any bears in the forest at all, let alone any coming out to meet me.

Our group abandoned this point and headed for a small observatory on the shores of the lake, electing to wait for bears to come out in search of the sockeye salmon they love so much. Before long, a bear appeared ahead of us, far in the distance. I decided I would try to call out to it and draw it closer using the power of Ki.

I continued to transmit Ki, and the exchange deepened. At first, the bear was jumping in and out of the water, trying to catch salmon but, after some time, it entered the forest. At that moment, I felt what I assumed to be the bodily information of the bear stream into me through my palm. My intuition told me that the bear was in a state of relaxation. However, the river between us was in spate, and we could not cross into the forest into which the bear had disappeared.

Thus, we were unable to confirm if that bear, in its state of relaxation, had fallen down or not. If the weather had been better, I really think that I would have been able to fell a bear. It was truly a shame. The Kamchatka peninsula is a low-pressure zone, and apparently it almost always is stormy, with very few days of good weather.

By afternoon, the rain and the wind had abated a bit, so we went by helicopter to Petropavlovsk-Kamchatsky Airport and returned to Khabarovsk on a domestic flight.

*The author and his party returning from the point from which he transmitted Ki into the forest in hopes of making the bear fall asleep.

The Siberian Tiger

On October 12th, our team walked through a conifer forest on the outskirts of Khabarovsk in search of the tiger said to be the strongest in the world: the Siberian tiger. However, we were unable to find one.

The next day, our guide introduced us to Mr. Yevgeny, a biologist. The guide asked Mr. Yevgeny if it would be okay for me to do my Ki energy showdown with one of the Siberian tigers he was monitoring for his research on the ecology and environmental preservation of the species. Mr. Yevgeny gladly agreed and promised us his assistance.

Finally, my showdown with a Siberian tiger had arrived. I entered a six-foot-by-six-foot cage in the corner of the forest. Standing in the middle of it, I aimed my right hand towards the depths of the forest and, waving it up and down, began to transmit Ki. I waited for the tiger for about ten minutes, transmitting Ki the whole time. At first, only one appeared from within the woods. It drew close to my cage, and began to pace around it, almost as if it was sizing me up. Then another one appeared. And, before I knew it, a third had appeared, and I found myself surrounded by three tigers. Trepidation raced through me.

After what felt like an eternity, one of the tigers growled, as if to scare off the other two. This was probably the strongest of the three, I thought. Perhaps it had decided that I was its food. In any case, it successfully intimidated and drove away the other two tigers. And so, it became a one-on-one showdown. When I went back to watch the whole thing, I found something I did not recall, and that was rather surprising. Whenever the tiger put its face close to the cage, I also put my face close to the cage. At times the distance between our faces was no more than about 30 cm.

Perhaps this was my own primal instinct spurring me to confront this threat. After some time, the tiger dropped its hindquarters and fell to the earth. However, it immediately raised its head up again, and so I decided to try for the first time a new technique I'd invented called "heaven-earth unification exchange."

First, one holds their palm very close to the ground, and very slowly traces three circles in the air. Then, they raise their hand above their head, and draw three circles in the air, just like a flying kite. Lastly, the individual points their palms towards the ground and lowers their hands. They will notice a feeling of compression in their palms, which grows much stronger after their hands pass their knee level. Repeat this process three times.

As I was trying this new method, when my hands reached my knee level for the third time, I felt a fierce compression sensation and an equally fierce feedback sensation. At the same time, the tiger before me plopped its head on the ground with an audible thud. It had become completely relaxed. It even raised its back legs, showing me its belly. It was acting just like a cat. Not long after, the other two also fell over near the cage. All three tigers were completely relaxed and even yawning.

Perhaps because the shadow of the cage prevented him from seeing the first tiger, Mr. Yevgeny declared that the animals were not completely relaxed because they'd not displayed their bellies. I was therefore made to have yet another showdown with these tigers.

Again, quite suddenly, a tiger appeared from within the forest, and behind it I glimpsed three others. They were gathered around a small pool of water about 20 meters away. I again began to perform heaven-earth unification exchange. And, after some time, I noticed the tigers falling, one by one, in the area around the pool. Additionally, the one that first appeared opened his hind legs, and gave me a full view of his belly.

Mr. Yevgeny, who had been watching all this, was well and truly surprised. This was yet another plain and clear display of the great power of Ki, made possible this time by heaven-earth unification exchange.

*Caption 1: Siberian tiger, approaching the cage containing the author

*Caption 2: The tiger fell over upon being sent Ki

Ki Discoveries through Exchanges with Animals

The series of phenomena that occurred during the Ki exchanges with animals allowed me to discover and prove the existence of Ki. This was an enormously important achievement for Kiryo. While most people have some dim awareness of the fact that the act of living is Ki itself, because they have always attempted to use accepted knowledge to understand it, they have been unable to do so.

However, it can easily be said that the series of phenomena that occurred in my Ki exchanges with animals wonderfully proved the existence of Ki. I would like to organize and explain these phenomena in further detail (refer to Table 1).

Let us start with the proof of Ki.

Back at the zoo, when I transmitted Ki to the gorilla, the gorilla responded to my Ki: it scratched its body, went to hide in the shadow of a nearby boulder, yawned and fell asleep. It is plausible to say that this incident is proof of the existence of Ki.

Table 1: Ki Discoveries through Exchanges with Animals

	Place	Animal	Ki Discovery
	Zoo	Gorilla	Proof of Ki

(Asahi TV)

	Place	Animal	Ki Discovery
Exposition	Australia	Elephant, bull (rodeo), kangaroo, koala, giant tortoise	Ki exchange sensation
Development	Spain	Fighting bull, sheep	Ki chain reaction
Climax	Kenya	Buffalo, topi, elephant, lion, cheetah, rhinoceros, hippo, zebra	Collective energy Relaxation space
Resolution	Siberia	Siberian tiger, (brown bear)	Heaven-earth unification exchange
			* A natural energy of the unification of heaven and earth. Kiryo involves becoming a medium for that energy.

Exposition: Australia

My Ki exchange experiences in Australia with the elephant, bull, and kangaroo serve as proof of the Ki exchange sensation. While there was some small amount of hand feedback sensation with the elephant and the kangaroo, it was with the bulls that the sensation was most clearly manifested. I became especially sure of its existence during my exchange with the fierce bull Viking.

While the five other bulls fell down with sole Kiryo, Viking was rather obstinate, and would not fall down, so I tried remote Kiryo on him.

While maintaining the Ki exchange sensation—that is, the connection sensation—I was experiencing with Viking, I moved about fifty meters away from him, continuing to transmit Ki the whole way. As a result, the waves from Viking suddenly became stronger and he fell down just when I thought he would.

Anyone can do this with many different kinds of animals; they need only master Ki energy. And the odd thing with Viking was that the farther away from him I got, the stronger my hand feedback sensation became. There was most likely something in between us that was amplifying my Ki energy. This sort of energy amplification was another important discovery made through this experience.

Development: Spain

My Ki exchange experiences in Spain with the sheep and the fighting bull serve as proof of the Ki chain reaction.

My Ki exchange with the sheep was done in the presence of over 300 animals. It was my first time exchanging Ki with so many at once. I sincerely doubt that a single person witnessing what happened expected that over a hundred of those sheep would fall down as they did. Why did these sheep fall down one after another?

I have coined a specific name for this phenomenon in Kiryo terminology: the Ki chain reaction. The Ki chain reaction refers to what happens when, after one being receives Ki, the Ki response travels to another being.

As whichever sheep in the herd was most easily influenced by Ki fell down first, that same response occurred in nearby sheep, and, one after another, it spread to the rest of the sheep in a response cascade. Eventually, this cascade caused enough sheep to fall down that it was as if a "carpet of sheep" had unrolled itself before me.

In the case of my showdown with the fighting bull, I continued to transmit Ki to the fighting bull Bogabante as he remained in the center of the arena from the upper levels of the stands. However, he was reacting even to the small sound of a person standing up; he simply refused to fall.

I remembered the Ki chain reaction that occurred with the sheep, and so we had three other bulls brought into the arena. Once Bogabante noticed that he was among friends, his wariness diminished, and he began to yawn. And even when a towel was waved in front of him, because he'd lost his warlike instincts, he actually retreated backwards. This is the opposite of how a fighting bull should react. It was truly a wonderful proof of the Ki chain reaction.

Climax: Kenya

My Ki exchange experiences in Kenya with the buffalo, topi, elephant, hippo, and zebra all serve as proof of the concepts of "collective energy" and "relaxation spaces."

Humans and animals alike possess living energy. When the living energies of individuals are collected in one place, they amplify each other and meld into one, and a strong single energy is born. We refer to this as "collective energy."

Relaxation spaces are healing spaces brought about by collective energy. Collective energy performs muscular adjustment and stimulates blood flow. Blood circulation to the brain is improved, and oxygen and nutrients are more readily provided to its cells. The brain is vitalized, and the resultant relaxed states of each individual create a healing space. We call this a "relaxation space."

I will explain these concepts further using the buffalo as an example.

The phenomenon that produced the spectacle of the buffalo falling down is the same as what occurred with the sheep: the Ki chain reaction.

The buffalo received the Ki I sent to them after becoming a medium for natural energy. Their individual energies responded to one another in a catenary fashion. These mutually interacting energies were amplified and collected together. That collective energy built a vast healing space on the great plains of Kenya. Inside this relaxation space, the wariness of the buffalo melted away, they entered a state of relaxation, and almost all of them fell asleep. The seven bulls that did not fall asleep were relaxed yet paralyzed—they could not move.

Resolution: Siberia

My Ki exchange experiences in Siberia with the Siberian tiger serve as proof of heaven-earth unification exchange.

The "heaven-earth unification" part of heaven-earth unification exchange refers to an energy that is the unification of the energies of heaven and earth. Heaven-earth unification exchange refers to the process by which people become mediums for that energy, and exchange it with each other.

Heaven-earth unification exchange can bring forth a very powerful energy. The reason for this is that all living things live amidst a unified energy of heaven and earth. The use of this energy is heaven-earth unification exchange. My showdown with the Siberian tiger was made possible by a very powerful heaven-earth unification exchange.

The Physiological Makeup of Animals

How did the power of Ki make all those animals fall down? The reason for their collapse is the existence of the twin sensory nerves (I will explain this concept in detail in a later chapter).

The physiological makeup of an animal refers to the structures of its body that allow it to remain alive and active. Kiryo focuses on the activity of the nerves as part of an animal's physiological makeup. The animals that fell down possessed normal sensory nerves, but, from the perspective of the world of Kiryo, they also possessed two additional sensory nerves. These are the Kiryo Nerve and the Wave Perception Nerve.

The Kiryo nerve uses the power of Ki to heal and prevent against illness and the like. The wave perception nerve perceives the great variety of waves that we can experience. It is believed that animals possess ten to a hundred times as many of this sort of nerve as do humans.

43

The world of animals is one of kill or be killed. In order for an animal to protect itself, its wave perception nerve, which perceives the great variety of waves that one can experience, is always awake and working. After receiving, the twin sensory nerves of the various animals I have been discussing till now responded very acutely. Additionally, their Kiryo nerves and wave perception nerves mutually activated. This causes muscular adjustment, which improves blood flow, allowing them to relax, their wariness to melt away, and ultimately causes them to fall down.

Chapter 2: Discovery of the Twin Sensory Nerves

From the Cognitive World to the Sensory

Establishment of the Kiryo Academy

On the 8th day of the 8th month of the 8th year of Heisei (August 8, 1996), I founded the Kiryo Academy. For many years, I had been implementing the techniques of Kiryo, and the fact that Ki energy has spectacular effects on illness and injury had already been proven. I knew that Ki exists everywhere, and that every living person possesses Ki. I had once thought that Ki was something everyone latently possessed, but I had realized that the act of living itself is Ki. This "life power" can be either weak, or it can be strong.

All one needs to do is draw forth and amplify this living Ki energy. However, people were ignorant both of the fact that they contained Ki within themselves, and that there exists a method to draw it forth. I opened the Kiryo Academy with the goal of communicating the wonder of this Ki energy—that is, Kiryo—to one and all.

Below are the ideas that formed the founding principles for the Kiryo Academy—the fundamental Kiryo effects.

1. Ki energy is natural healing power.

45

2. Ki energy has pain-Killing properties.
3. Ki energy can only benefit, and cannot harm.
4. Ki energy-cured sicknesses do not often reappear.
5. Ki energy returns one to their original, natural state of health.
6. Ki energy improves the function of the brain and the nerves of the entire body.
7. Ki energy accelerates convalescence.
8. Ki energy is beneficial for health, longevity, and beauty.
9. Ki energy is especially effective on the brain.

This last point is particularly important. Because in modern humans, the brainstem—the source of our bodies' life-preserving activities—is especially weak, our society has many ill and near-ill people. Kiryo has the ability to vitalize the brainstem.

On November 9th, 1996, our first class was held, and the mastery of Ki energy began. There were only about seven or eight students at the time, and the class mainly focused on two-person Kiryo methods. The class soon increased to 30 students.

At the start of 1997, preparations were made to open a branch of the school in Kyoto, and on February 16th, it finally happened. There were about five or six students total. Things went smoothly at both the main school in the south of Aoyama and the Kyoto branch until the end of March.

However, at that time, the number of students began to gradually decline. I had absolutely no idea why this was happening. However, I knew that shutting the new schools would be an inexcusable affront to the students that were continuing to attend.

I spent days wrestling with this problem. On one such day, a student came up to me and casually commented that many of the students that left had complained that, "Kiryo has no theory." The moment I heard this, I had a realization. I realized that Kiryo had no way of explaining itself. I realized that I had arrogantly thought that because mastery of Ki energy and perceptive/differentiative ability was enough to heal oneself, it should be enough for anyone interested in Kiryo.

In other words, I understood that "being able to perform Kiryo", and "understanding and therefore becoming able to perform Kiryo" were two different things. So, how was I to get my students to understand Kiryo? I initially thought that there was no way. The world of Kiryo is a "sensory world," and no words to express this world had ever existed. I realized that I would have create, one by one, words to help people understand the world of Kiryo.

Pain and Pain-Like Sensations

First and foremost, let me make clear the fact that the sensation we feel in our palm is what allows us to experience the existence of Ki. This is the true nature of Ki. I decided to begin my endeavor by verbally expressing this sensation.

Truth be told, I had for some time been jotting down the sensory and onomatopoeic words people had been using to express these sensations. The first time that I experienced this feeling in my palms, it was a cool, blowing feeling. When the Kiryo recipient receives Kiryo, they feel something in their palm. And when the Kiryo practitioner puts their hand over the receiver's affected area, they feel a recovery reaction in the palm. When two people exchange Ki from palm to palm, they feel something. These multifarious wave sensations are referred to as hand feedback sensations. Everyone has these hand feedback sensations. It is quite easy to draw out, amplify, and master them.

Next, I would like to offer an at-a-glance table of the sensory and onomatopoeic words people have used to verbalize these sensations.

How best could I collectively characterize these sensory and onomatopoeic terms?

In my experience, the strongest sensation I initially felt in my palm was when I placed it about four inches away from my mother's stomach. I suddenly felt pain as if long nails were being driven through my hand.

Table 2:Types of Hand Feedback Sensations at a Glance

Sensory Word	Onomatopoeic Words	
Stiffness	oomph-oomph	prickle-prickle
Heat	fwoo-fwoo	bzzt-bzzt
Warmth	crackle-crackle	unff-unff
Numbness	twitch-twitch	fluff-fluff
Ball-like	sparkle-sparkle	phew-phew
Pressure	sizzle-sizzle	thump-thump
Compression	throb-throb	whump-whump
Contraction	wrinkle-wrinkle	scrape-scrape
Tactile	zuuuun	fwaaaa
Lukewarm	thud-thud	bubble-bubble
Fuzziness	lubb-lubb	itchy-itchy
Tickling	achy-achy	slink-slink
Windy	burn-burn	zhoop-zhoop
StroKing	pet-pet	rub-rub
Pulling	yank-yank	rustle-rustle
Weight	boing-boing	
Sunburn-like		
Cold		

In fact, the pain was so excessive that my hand instinctively flew backward. Thus, I named these feelings "pain sensations." However, I later learned that many Academy students did not feel anything like these pain sensations in their palms.

Thus, I drew on my experience once again, and thought of how my first sensation was a cool, blowing feeling, and named weak hand feedback sensations "pain-like sensations." Now, all sensations felt in the palm of the hand, from the faint and weak to the powerfully excruciating, could be referred to by the collective name of "pain and pain-like sensations."

These were the first words of Kiryo terminology. The pain and pain-like sensations allow us to experience the fact that Ki energy is existence itself. Additionally, they prove that everything possesses Ki.

From the Cognitive World to the Sensory

As the first word of Kiryo terminology, establishing that the sensations felt in the palm were known as "pain and pain-like sensations" was an enormously significant first step towards the eventual goal of understanding the world of Kiryo. Kiryo is a world where Ki is understood solely through sensory means. Therefore, in order to take yet another step into this sensory world, I will now introduce two new terms: the "Ki Response Sensation," and the "Twin Sensory Nerves."

The Ki Response Sensation refers to the sensation felt when responding to Ki in a "feel as you are" state. Depending on the part of the body that responds, one may refer to a "hand feedback sensation," a "foot feedback sensation" or a "body feedback sensation." These are our so-called entryways into the world of Ki.

Figure 1: The Sensory World

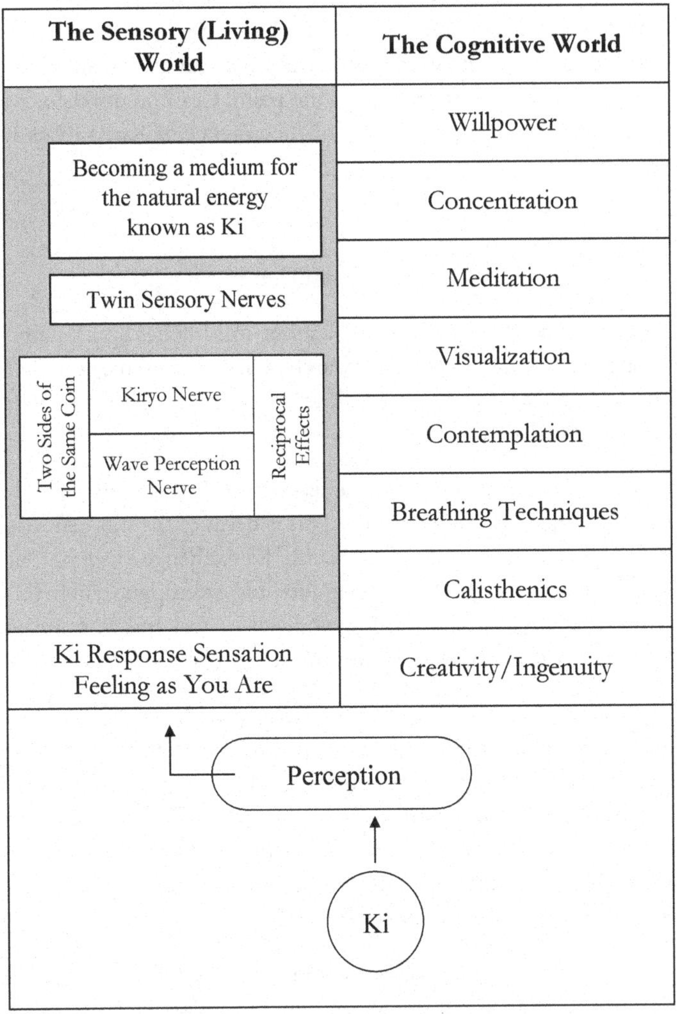

The Sensory (Living) World	The Cognitive World
	Willpower
Becoming a medium for the natural energy known as Ki	Concentration
	Meditation
Twin Sensory Nerves	
	Visualization
Two Sides of the Same Coin / Kiryo Nerve / Wave Perception Nerve / Reciprocal Effects	Contemplation
	Breathing Techniques
	Calisthenics
Ki Response Sensation Feeling as You Are	Creativity/Ingenuity
Perception ← / Ki →	

The Twin Sensory Nerves are the Kiryo Nerve and the Wave Perception Nerve. I will describe them using the previous diagram (refer to Figure 1). The Ki Response Sensation is our entryway to the sensory world. I will focus my explanations on hand feedback sensations felt in the palm. Configurations using the hand are also the beginning of the practice of Kiryo mastery (exercise).

Kiryo Exercise: Palm Gap Exchange

Hold your hands in front of you about four inches apart, palms facing each other. Place your awareness in your palms, and once you feel something, just allow yourself to feel it. The "something" you feel is Ki.

Even if you can't immediately feel Ki, you will certainly become able to do so over time. This is because the moment you place your awareness in your palms, Ki exchange begins. One need not use creativity and ingenuity and attempt to enter this world cognitively. Simply allow yourself to feel and respond to Ki as you are, and you will enter the sensory world.

Because healthy people have good Ki balance, it is actually more difficult for them to perceive Ki. On the contrary, sick people, because they thirst for Ki, can manifest hand feedback sensations more quickly. Persistently continuing to practice Kiryo exercises is what is most important. Everyone possesses the ability to manifest Ki response sensations; some just feel them faster or slower than others.

The Ki response sensation awakens the twin sensory nerves. As the Kiryo response sensation gradually becomes stronger, the twin sensory nerves begin to function.

The twin sensory nerves are what together become a medium for the natural energy known as Ki—they are healing nerves. In order to allow them to become mediums for this natural energy, one need only awaken them by feeling as one is. Once they have been awakened, one of the twin sensory nerves—the wave perception nerve—allows us to feel Ki in our palms as the pain and pain-like sensations. These hand feedback sensations are manifestations of our perceptive/differentiative ability.

The Kiryo nerve is awakened at the same time as the wave perception nerve. The Kiryo nerve cannot, on its own, enable the detection of Ki as the hand feedback sensation. Only once the wave perception nerve has been awakened can one experience the fact that Ki is existence itself. This is Ki energy, brought forth by the Kiryo nerve.

The Kiryo nerve and the wave perception nerve are a pair, they are two sides of the same coin, and they act reciprocally. Awakening of the twin sensory nerves allows for the mastery of Ki energy and perceptive/differentiative ability.

Discovery of the Twin Sensory Nerves

Kiryo Focuses on Nervous Activity

Our nerves preside over all our bodily functions, from the cognitive to the life-preserving. Even in our battles with illness, nerves play an important role.

The word "nerve" in Japanese, "shinkei," was coined by Genpaku Sugita, a scholar of Dutch medicine who lived in the middle Edo period. Genpaku, while translating a Dutch medical text he called "New Text on Anatomy," came up with the term during his translation. Apparently, he coined it from the characters used to write the words "divine energy" (a force that makes up all things) and "vessel" (the term used for the blood vessels of the human body).

The text treats "divine energy" as the concept that Ki is the foundation for all things in the universe and "vessels" as composed of the blood and the vessels that carry it—both things indispensable to the human body. I focused on the activity of the nerves while being completely ignorant of this definition, and was surprised to find out that it and my own conceptions aligned so closely, especially considering its use in Kiryo.

The first character of "shinkei" is "shin," which refers to the universe (nature), while the second character, "kei," refers to the human body. Thus, "nerve" signifies both the universe (nature) and the human body. A spectacularly important word indeed.

I was surprised that the concept of Ki was so central to the concept of the nerve itself. It aligns closely with the precepts of Kiryo outlined in the Kiryo mastery texts contained at the Academy, like "Kiryo is being in a natural state," and "Kiryo is becoming a medium for natural energy." The existence and functions of the sensory nerves are vital in experiencing the natural energy known as Ki. To Kiryo, the existence and functions of the sensory nerves are indispensable.

Let us focus on the bodily aspect of the idea of the nerve, and consider its commonalities with the teachings of Kiryo. In the Kiryo Academy, we always check the pulse at the wrist and identify changes in its beating pattern before and after Kiryo exercise. Even during our master's courses, before beginning our exercises, we randomly pair off and check each other's pulses. And after we are done, we check both our own and our partner's pulses.

Five changes are evidenced in the pulse upon completion of Kiryo exercise: it becomes composed, firm, strong, plump, and soft. These are indicative of the fact that Ki energy has made blood circulation inside the body good and proper. It is this blood circulation which heals illness and injury, and also prevents illness from occurring.

I am still surprised by how much commonality there is between the meaning of the word nerve and the practically-determined nervous function focused on in Kiryo.

Kiryo understands Ki through the sensory world. Thus, I would like to begin our journey into the sensory world with the basics of the existence and functions of the sensory nerves.

I have previously explained how a lack of words and explanations during the education and training of students at the Academy very nearly led to its closing down. It became clear to me and others that expressing the essence of Kiryo with existing vocabulary was exceedingly difficult. The only path available to us was to understand the essence of Kiryo through sensory nerve function and verbalize new words to describe that understanding.

I realized that in the world of Kiryo, there existed two new, previously unknown nerves that performed vitally important functions. Discovering and naming these twin sensory nerves elucidated the sensory world of Kiryo, and made communicating its truths possible to others. In addition, it helped us verbalize the various sensory phenomena that occur.

The Discovery and Naming of the Twin Sensory Nerves

The nerves of the human body consist of the central nerves (the brain and spinal cord) and the peripheral nerves that connect them to the parts of the body (the skin, the sensory organs, the muscles, the glands, etc.). The peripheral nerves can be further divided, based on their functions, into the motor nerves, the sensory nerves, and the autonomic nerves. From the perspective of Kiryo, the sensory and autonomic nerves are most important among these.

As some may already know, the bodies of humans and animals possess various sensory organs (for sight, sound, smell, taste, and touch).

Within these five sensory organs, there are sensory cells and sensory nerves. A "sensory cell" refers to a cell that has the ability to generate an action potential across its membrane upon receiving a stimulus. These cells receive stimuli from the outside world and transmit them to the sensory nerves. The sensory nerves transmit the stimuli of the sensory cells to the central nervous system. In this way, the sensory organs, sensory cells, and sensory nerves operate in collaboration, transmitting stimulation to the central nerves. We are able to virtually instantaneously respond to or differentiate between these stimuli and act accordingly.

As I mentioned earlier, in the Kiryo world, two new sensory nerves exist, and they have vitally important functions. These are the Kiryo Nerve and the Wave Perception Nerve. The Kiryo nerve, is the nerve which heals illness and injury using Ki energy. The wave perception nerve perceives and differentiates the various waveforms of the outside world.

From the perspective of Kiryo, these twin sensory nerves exist alongside the five sensory nerves. It is simply that we do not normally notice them.

In the primeval era, in order to protect us from external threats, it is thought that the wave perception nerve functioned exceedingly sensitively. With the growth of the cerebrum our cognitive abilities developed. We invented habits and tools for protecting ourselves, and the wave perception nerve's function gradually lessened, eventually falling to the level it is at in the modern era.

The healthier someone is, the stronger their Kiryo nerve functions. Because Ki is existence itself, the Kiryo nerve functions within and as a part of that existence. I will elaborate on the reciprocal effects of the twin sensory nerves later.

The event that first spurred my entry into the world of Kiryo was the electric shock (discussed in great detail in the previously-published *Kiryo*) that occurred as I was sleeping soundly in the middle of the night.

This electric shock happened as follows: I awoke suddenly from a deep sleep and heard a "thud" sound in my head. I thought a car accident or something of the sort had happened outside. As I tried to get up out of bed, tingling, vibrating shockwaves raced through my body. I felt a second bout of shockwaves immediately after the first. I somehow managed to fall asleep, but over the next few days, I had four more such shocks.

With regards to the "thud" sound I heard in my head, I believe that that was me noticing a change happening at the microscopic level in my brain. For example, people who have experienced subarachnoid hemorrhages describe feeling as though they were suddenly struck with a hammer, hearing a "thud" sound in their heads, and then losing consciousness.

This is what we know to happen in cranial illnesses like subarachnoid hemorrhages. However, in my case, I believe a microscopic change took place inside my brain cells, which then burgeoned into the huge shockwave sensation I felt throughout my body. So, what exactly presented this microscopic stimulus to my brain? I believe it was the work of the sensory cells of my twin sensory nerves.

Specifically, these sensory cells received some kind of internal or external stimulation and awakened my wave perception nerve. When you enter into sleep, your brainstem becomes briskly active in order to heal your tired body and its

57

illnesses. In fact, one can differentiate when exactly someone falls asleep by placing their palm over that person's head; the moment that person slips into sleep, the hand feedback sensation in the other person's palm will suddenly get stronger. Thus, when I fell into a deep sleep, and my brainstem briskly activated, my sensory cells were both internally and externally stimulated. That stimulation was channeled to the wave perception nerve and transmitted to the central sensory organ within my brain stem. And at that moment, I felt those shockwaves race through my body. The wave perception nerve encompasses the entire body. It reaches even into the internal organs.

Approximately three months after the shock, I had to photocopy some documents. After I pressed start on the copier, it started to move from side-to-side. Strangely, I started to feel that movement in my stomach! My internal organs had perceived the movement of the copier.

The wave perception nerve possesses the ability to detect all kinds of waves: changes in the internal information of animals and people, the waveforms of plants and precious gems, invisible wave energy, etc. The more one uses this ability, the better it gets. Eventually, one will grow to be able to strongly feel with their palms and soles, and will become able to experience the fact that Ki is existence itself.

The Kiryo nerve is the one that heals illness and injury. It forms a pair with the wave perception nerve, and the two operate reciprocally.

After my wave perception shock, I recovered my health through the use of Ki energy. Up until that point, I had suffered from low blood pressure, catarrhal inflammation of the stomach, stomach pain, hemorrhoids, headaches, tonsillitis, inner ear inflammation, and cold urticaria, among other things. My illnesses were all swept away, and I was returned to a state of health, all thanks to the power of Ki.

As I have explained before, over the years, many thousands of people have learned Kiryo. Among them, some have realized the true effectiveness of Ki energy. During the Kiryo mastery courses at the academy, most students are able to master Ki after only 50 weekly lessons.

Incidentally, what exactly senses and transmits this Ki energy that we experience? I believe it is only possible for this to be the work of our nerves. Nerves are bundles of fibers that transmit excitatory and stimulatory impulses. One of the fibers in these bundles performs the function of sensing and transmitting Ki energy, and using it to heal the body. That is why I decided to name structures responsible for performing these functions the "Kiryo nerve" and the "wave perception nerve."

Reciprocal Effects of the Twin Sensory Nerves

I have explained quite a bit about the twin sensory nerves, but I have not mentioned the following: just as "Ki is existence itself," so too are the twin sensory nerves existence itself. Here, I would like to use my own experiences to describe the reciprocal effects of the twin sensory nerves.

The first sort of hand feedback sensation I felt through my wave perception nerve was a cool, blowing feeling. I was treating my father, who had been complaining of a pain emanating from his shoulder. Rather unbelievably, I actually managed to cure him. That was the beginning of my Kiryo career. Later on, while trying to heal my mother's stomach pain, I placed my hand over her stomach and suddenly felt an intense pain in my palm. In fact, it was enough to make me raise my hand above my head. This was my first Kiryo pain sensation.

About two years after my wave perception shock experience, a woman (26 at the time) who was suffering from severe depression visited my house for treatment. I had her lie on her back, face up, and I placed my hand above the crown of her head. The moment I began to wave it up and down, her face twisted into a terrible scowl and she began to thrash around violently. To prevent her from getting up or injuring herself, I asked her mother to hold her down, and I performed Kiryo on her for about an hour. It felt as if I was fighting with her. Throughout this time, I felt a variety of noisy, murky hand feedback sensations.

All of a sudden, those murky sensations disappeared, and my palm was without any sensation whatsoever. Simultaneously, the woman, who had only a moment ago been writhing around, grew still. Before long, she came to, stood up, and looked around nervously. That terrible scowl was gone, and before me stood an elegant, refined woman. It was almost as if an evil spirit had been exorcised from her.

The woman exclaimed, "The boulders I've been carrying on my back have vanished! The fog has cleared!" The depression that had plagued her for over eight years had been driven away in just one session. The woman's Kiryo nerve had healed her sickness, and her wave perception nerve, differentiating this change, had conveyed that information to my palm.

I'd proven the fact that the hands possess perceptive and differentiative ability as well as the existence of the wave perception nerve itself. This was my first experience with perceptive and differentiative ability.

Next, I would like to return to the topics of Chapter 1 and describe how my twin sensory nerves were functioning during my Ki exchanges with those animals.

All these exchanges begin with me sending Ki to the animals. Upon doing this, my Kiryo nerve starts to function. At the same time, my wave perception nerve also starts to function. As the animals receive my Ki, they feel it with their wave perception nerves, and their Kiryo nerves begin to awaken. The Ki energy these animals have received is instantaneously transmitted to and stimulates their brainstems, which then sends orders to the autonomic nerves.

The autonomic nerves promote adjustment of the visceral and skeletal muscles, which causes them to relax.

Blood flow adjustment then occurs, promoting proper blood flow. When blood circulation becomes good and proper, blood is better provided to the brain, and the brain stem is activated.

As the animals blood circulation improved, they fell into a relaxed state and their life energies increase. Information about changes that occur in the animals is transmitted as bodily information to my wave perception nerve in my palm. I continue to send Ki to them, and once the animals reach a peak state of relaxation, they fall down. At that moment, I feel a strong shock in my palm.

I realized through my exchanges with animals that the function of the wave perception nerves in animals is incomparably greater than that of humans.

Why is it that despite their strong healing powers, the existence of the twin sensory nerves has not, till now, been acknowledged?

To help answer this question, please look at, "Figure 2: Illness and Nervous Function" below.

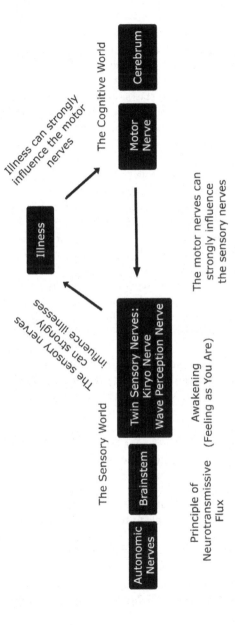

Figure 2: Illness and Nervous Function

Illness, the motor nerves, and the twin sensory nerves exist in a triangular relationship. First, illness is capable of strongly influencing the motor nerves and the cerebrum. This because they are not healing nerves. On the other hand, the motor nerves are capable of acting strongly on the twin sensory nerves. In fact, the reason we ask people to lie down during Kiryo is so that their muscles can rest and not have to work to keep them balanced—we do not want their motor nerves to be active during the Kiryo process.

By doing this, the Kiryo recipient becomes able to feel the flow of Ki with their weakly active wave perception nerve. Because the twin sensory nerves are weaker than the motor nerves, moving, walking, or running will not give the twin sensory nerves a chance to go to work. This is one reason why people do not normally sense the existence of Ki energy.

The twin sensory nerves are capable of manifesting incredibly strong healing powers on illnesses. Awakening one's twin sensory nerves through "feeling as they are," vitalization of the brainstem begins, and the autonomic nerves start to function. As a result, the principle of neurotransmissive flux (explained later) comes into play. Adjustment of mind and body is thereby carried out, and we become able to defeat our illnesses. Having defeated whatever illnesses plague us, the twin sensory nerves are able to help the weakened motor nerves as well.

Awaken the Twin Sensory Nerves

The activity of our nerves keeps us alive. If our nerves function properly, we are able to remain healthy; if they do not, we fall ill.

Kiryo involves using the nerves to comprehend Ki, to feel its exchange and flow. This exchange and flow is neurotransmissive exchange. Mutual awakening of the twin sensory nerves is the beginning of neurotransmissive exchange.

Our twin sensory nerves allow us to be aware of the strength of Ki.

For example, if you place your hands about four inches apart, and, keeping them in line with each other, continue to widen the gap between them, and finally begin moving them up and down once they are about six inches apart, you will begin to feel a cool sensation, quite like that of air passing against your skin. This is a sensory phenomenon caused by the mutual awakening of the twin sensory nerves in your left and right palms.

The Relationship between Ki, the Nerves, and the Blood

Humans live within an energy that is the unification of terrestrial and atmospheric energies. The unification of the energies of heaven and earth. In Kiryo, we refer to this idea by stating that humans live inside "the natural energy known as Ki." The existence of Ki is comprehended with the twin sensory nerves, which allowing each of us to become a medium for the natural energy known as Ki. By becoming a medium for it, one is able to master Ki energy itself.

Once the twin sensory nerves are awakened, the other nerves of the body respond and are vitalized as well. In particular, the autonomic nervous system is energized. As explained before, when the mastery courses at the academy are held, the first thing that is done in each class is the checking of one's pulse. As students recheck their pulse after finishing their class, without exception, they find that their pulses have changed in ways I am about to explain.

The following changes are observed: due to the vitalization of the sympathetic arm of the autonomic nervous system, the pulse is "firm," "strong," and "plump," and due to the vitalization of the parasympathetic nerves, the pulse is also "composed" and "supple."

Regarding the blood, it provides oxygen, nutrients, hormones, and antibodies to every corner of the body. It also carries away waste products like carbon dioxide. The nerves, in particular, require sufficient nutrients and oxygen.

The twin sensory nerves are the same. Once blood circulation improves, the nerves of the brain and body are vitalized. This further improves blood flow.

We often do the following in the mastery courses at the academy: one person in a pair of facing partners places one of their hands above the joined, outstretched hands of his or her partner. Very soon after the person with the single hand placed above those of the other begins to shake his or her hand back and forth, the outstretched palms of the partner will redden, and red and white spots can be seen on them. This is because the twin sensory nerves in the palms of the individual with both of his or her hands outstretched have been stimulated, and blood has collected in them. This phenomenon is proof of the existence of the power of Ki, and therefore proof of the existence of the twin sensory nerves. When looking at the palms of an individual that has mastered the power of Ki through the mastery course at the academy, they appear to be soft, supple, and plump. This is proof of the fact that blood has collected in them, rejuvenating the cells therein.

Additionally, if one receives Ki into the head while lying down, blood is brought to the brain and it is vitalized. Consequently, the blood vessels of the brain soften, which helps greatly in preventing things like cerebral hemorrhage, cerebral infarct, and dementia.

With the relationship between Ki, the nerves, and the blood discussed above serving as a foundation, let us explore the idea of neurotransmissive flux in Kiryo.

The Principle of Neurotransmissive Flux

Please refer to Diagram 3: "The Principle of Neurotransmissive Flux."

The centerpoint of Kiryo itself lies in the brainstem. The brainstem is the backbone that supports the most fundamental life functions—respiration, cardiac activity, temperature maintenance, among others. The twin sensory nerves are also controlled by the brainstem. Thus, let us investigate, from the perspective of Kiryo, the function of the brainstem and subsequently that of the autonomic nervous system. (ref. "A

66

Dictionary for Understanding the Organization and Function of the Body," Kansai Corp., 2002, ed. Tooru Mori).

The brain is contained inside the cranium, and it continues down into the spinal cord. Four parts make up the brainstem, in the following order, from the bottom up: the medulla oblongata, the pons, the mesencephalon, and the diencephalon. The brainstem is also the tube through which the neural fibers that connect the brain to the rest of the body pass.

The diencephalon contains the thalamus and hypothalamus. The thalamus transmits the information it receives from the sensory nerves to the rest of the body. The hypothalamus is the central organ of the autonomic nervous system, and it regulates things like temperature regulation, sleep, and reproduction.

The mesencephalon regulates the senses of sight and hearing and also functions to preserves the muscles and posture of the body.

The pons contains the seats of processes like respiration, circulation, and deglutition (swallowing). Additionally, both the facial nerve, which moves the face and eyes, and the trigeminal nerve come out of the pons.

Diagram 3: The Principle of Neurotransmissive Flux

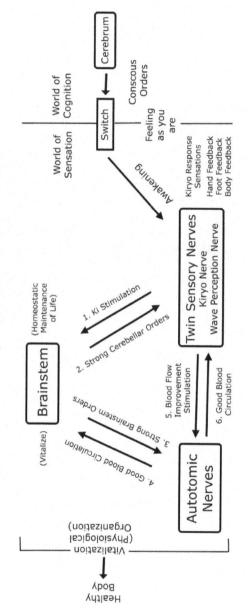

The seats of many important life-preserving functions lie in the medulla oblongata. Nerves like the vagus, the sublingual, and the glossopharyngeal originate here. This region is the seat of many functions, including respiration, cardiac function, blood circulation, digestion, metabolism, deglutition (swallowing), mastication (chewing), emesis, and coughing.

Next come the autonomic nerves. The autonomic nerves automatically regulate the function of the various types of organs of one's body independently of one's will. For example, this is why we cannot consciously will our hearts to stop beating.

The autonomic nervous system contains two subdivisions: the sympathetic and the parasympathetic. These two systems counteract one another. When the sympathetic nervous system is vitalized, the activity of the heart is increased, and the activity of the digestive system is slowed. In contrast, when the parasympathetic nervous system is vitalized, the activity of the heart is slowed, and the activity of the digestive system is increased.

The central seat of the sympathetic nervous system is in the spinal cord. The neural fibers of the spinal cord exit the spine and enter the sympathetic nerve trunks on either side of it. The peripheral nerves that exit these trunks spread to, among other things, all organs, the secretory glands, blood vessels, the skin, and sweat glands. The central seat of the parasympathetic nervous system is in the brainstem. It passes through the same path as the cranial nerves and spreads throughout the body in the same way as the sympathetic nervous system.

I would like to follow the layout of Diagram 3 and explain items (1) through (6). However, before doing so, let us try a simple exercise. First, separate your right and left palms by about four inches. This exercise is known as single-person "Palm Gap Adjustment Exchange." It is a configuration of Kiryo mastery (exercise) fundamental to the practice of Kiryo itself. If one places one's right and left palms completely together so they are touching, the touching feeling becomes stronger and we become unable to sense the flowing Ki. However, this four-inch gap invites us into the world of sensation, that is, the wonderful world of healing.

Allow your awareness to rest in your separated hands (4-inch gap). This is a conscious command given by your cerebrum. This conscious order allows us to take the first step from the world of cognition into the world of sensation.

After doing this, all you need to allow yourself to feel the Kiryo response sensations is to be as you are. Even if you are initially unable to feel them, if you continue practicing, you will gradually become able to feel them. This is because even if we cannot feel it, by doing Kiryo exercise, Ki exchange is taking place. Incidentally, it is difficult for a healthy person to sense this, and it is easier for an ill person; this is because the ill person is in a state of desiring Ki.

Upon entering the "feel as you are" state, the twin sensory nerves in both your left and right palms will be awakened. At the same time, the twin sensory nerves in your left and right palms will awaken each other, and begin neurotransmissive exchange.

(1) Ki Stimulation: From the Twin Sensory Nerves to the Brainstem

By becoming a medium for the natural energy known as Ki, and by awakening our twin sensory nerves, the brainstem immediately receives Ki stimulation and begins to work. The brainstem transmits signals from the twin sensory nerves to the cerebrum and cerebellum.

The brainstem itself is responsible for homeostatic maintenance of life. Homeostatic maintenance of life refers to the life force that constantly tells us to "live on, live on!" Kiryo will heighten this life force through the power of Ki; this process is known as "vitalization of the brainstem," and is an important focus of Kiryo.

(2) From the Brainstem to the Twin Sensory Nerves: Strong Cerebellar Orders

A vitalized brainstem sends strong orders in the opposite direction, back towards the twin sensory nerves. Because the twin sensory nerves are governed by the brainstem, this order causes them to begin to work. This is called the "vitalization of the twin sensory nerves." In other words, the brainstem and twin sensory nerves vitalize each other in response to Ki stimulation. I would like to introduce to you all an absolutely remarkable real-life example of this phenomenon.

The Ki power and perceptive/differentiative ability taught in the mastery courses at the academy, once mastered, do not go away. In fact, they continue to improve and magnify. Even if something were to happen, and you were forced to leave the academy for three years, your capability would not decrease. In fact, that ability would continue to increase. Why is this?

The truth lies in the vitalization of the brainstem. More specifically, it lies in the properties of homeostatic maintenance of life carried out by the brainstem that I just discussed. The strong brainstem orders that constantly, without pause, tell you to "live on, live on" are what vitalize the twin sensory nerves.

Our twin sensory nerves will be vitalized until the day we cease to live. Despite what our usual sensibilities would lead us to think, it is not possible to "use up" all of our Ki, nor can it "run out."

(3) From the Brainstem to the Autonomic Nervous System: Strong Brainstem Orders

Upon being vitalized by the receiving of a Ki stimulus from the twin sensory nerves, the brainstem sends strong orders to the autonomic nervous system. Receiving these strong orders causes the autonomic nervous system to begin working, and it itself is vitalized. The autonomic nervous system is the set of nerves that maintains life upon receiving orders from the brainstem. It maintains the homeostatic "live on" life force of the brainstem. Finally, the sympathetic and parasympathetic divisions of the autonomic nervous system receive these strong orders from the brainstem, and as a result, they are adjusted to be in harmonious balance and are vitalized.

When these nerves are unable to perform their work, autonomic dysfunction results, and a number of symptoms are brought about. Mentally, we suffer from unease, depression, loss of focus, loss of motivation, and feelings of loneliness, among other things. Physically, we suffer from a sense of malaise, dizziness, hot flashes, lack of appetite, and difficulty sleeping.

A weakening of the activity of the brainstem is what causes these symptoms of body and mind. Often, our current society is called a "stress society." The excessive amounts of stress we are surrounded with may yet be what is weakening that very source of our life, the activity of our brainstem.

(4) Good Blood Circulation: From the Autonomic Nerves to the Brainstem

Upon receiving strong orders from the brainstem, the autonomic nerves respond immediately and adjust the muscles throughout the body, promoting good blood flow.

Muscular adjustment is a process carried about by the autonomic nervous system after it has received strong orders from the brainstem whose purpose is to improve blood circulation; it specifically refers to the skeletal and visceral muscular adjustment that is conducted to achieve good blood flow. This is because the blood pumped out of the heart is circulated via the activity of the skeletal and visceral muscles throughout the body.

When blood circulation is improved, blood flows into the brain freely. And the brain, now fully provided with blood, is vitalized. Consequently, even stronger orders are sent to the autonomic and twin sensory nerves.

(5) Blood Flow Improvement Stimulation: From the Twin Sensory Nerves to the Autonomic Nerves

The twin sensory nerves also connect to the autonomic nerves, and can act upon the physiological framework underlying life. The autonomic nerves receive blood flow improvement stimulation from the twin sensory nerves.

(6) Good Blood Circulation: From the Autonomic Nerves to the Twin Sensory Nerves

After receiving blood flow improvement stimulation from the twin sensory nerves, the autonomic nerves provide blood to the twin sensory nerves spread throughout the body. After they receive this blood, the twin sensory nerves further vitalize.

The above are the fundamental principles that underlie neurotransmissive flux, which themselves form the central pillar of Kiryo. Below is a summary of the most critical points.

First, the conscious orders of the cerebrum cause our awareness to be placed in our palms as we perform palm gap adjustment exchange. The moment we allow our awareness to rest here, we switch from the world of cognition to the world of sensation. Next, in accordance with the Kiryo response sensations, we allow ourselves to feel as we are, and thereby awaken our twin sensory nerves. Once the twin sensory nerves are awakened, neurotransmissive flux begins to occur between the twin sensory nerves, the brainstem, and the autonomic nerves. The beginning of neurotransmissive flux between these structures allows for the vitalization of the physiological framework of our bodies.

Continuing Kiryo exercise allows us to further heighten our already existing neurotransmissive flux. The homeostatic vital maintenance function of our brainstems is vitalized, enabling the brainstem to continue to transmit strong orders. Further, adjustment of body and mind (adjustment of body and mind refers to muscular adjustment, blood flow adjustment, hormonal adjustment, immune adjustment, and psychological adjustment) is carried out. This adjustment of body and mind allows for the healing of mental and physical ailments, and is even capable of prematurely preventing illness from occurring.

Chapter 3: Kiryo Mastery (Exercise)

The Origin of Kiryo

I have already explained how wave perception shock was the impetus that spurred me to enter the world of Kiryo. As someone that had lived a very normal life until that point, I was quite bewildered by this world of Ki. However, the simple question of what exactly the "cool, blowing feeling" I could perceive in my hands was not answered. Intrigued by this phenomenon, I would try to concentrate my awareness on my hands, and when doing so, I was always able to feel this cool, blowing feeling.

Eventually, the cool, blowing feeling in my palms grew stronger, and along with it, my able to concentrate my awareness on my hands also grew, and it changed into an ability to place my awareness, for some time, in my palms. In an almost playful way, I would try opening and closing my hands by moving them to the right or left, and would enjoy the resulting feelings of stretching and compression. This practice eventually became a habitual part of my daily activities, and for near two years, I would, wherever and whenever I could, enjoy that cool, blowing feeling. All of this became the origin of the "feel as you are" concept we have in Kiryo today.

In the world of "feeling as you are," there is no need to strive to be original or creative. The process really is just "feeling as you are." "Feeling as you are" is what allows you to become a medium for the natural energy known as Ki. There is no other way to become a medium for the natural energy known as Ki aside from allowing yourself to feel as you are.

It is difficult to consciously attempt to grab hold of and control the vastness of Ki. The discovery of the "feel as you are" method was a momentous development in Kiryo theory. It is the origin of the practice. It is everything.

Finally, when this "feel as you are" practice awakens the twin sensory nerves, and the principle of neurotransmissive flux begins to work, the ill are healed, the healthy grow healthier, and even illnesses yet to come can be prevented.

Kiryo is Based in the Practice of Healing

After being awakened to the idea of Ki, I read many books on the subject, gaining knowledge of Ki from a variety of angles. Eventually, I began to think that I might be able to heal illnesses and injuries with the power of Ki.

I tried to do so for the first time on the pain my father was experiencing in his left shoulder. I faced the affected shoulder, placed my palm about four inches away from it, and tried waving it left and right. Waving one's palm left and right allows you to better feel the hand feedback sensation. After I felt I had done enough, I stopped, and asked my father how his shoulder pain felt. My father tried moving his shoulder and then exclaimed in surprise, "Wow! It doesn't hurt. That's so strange!"

The next morning, I asked my father again how he was feeling, and he moved his shoulder again, and said, "It doesn't hurt at all!" Even now, I remember this scene as if it were but yesterday.

I made a discovery here. I realized that when healing someone's affected area, one must face the affected area, hold one's palm about four inches away from it, and wave it back and forth several times. In Kiryo, we call this "hand-waving." By performing hand-waving, we can use the power of Ki to stimulate the affected region, and the restorative reaction can more easily be transmitted to the Kiryo practitioner in the form of the hand feedback sensation. Hand-waving is one of the most basic movements in Kiryo.

We can presume that in the case of my father's shoulder, the power of the Ki I sent to him awakened his twin sensory nerves, causing muscular and blood flow adjustment, which stimulated the Kiryo nerves and caused the pain to disappear.

This is how the Ki energy as elicited by Kiryo can have unparalleled pain-killing effects. After this incident, I continued, for the next two to three years, to practice my healing.

I became curious as to how the people I had healed went on to live their lives. Upon asking, I learned that almost all of them had completely forgotten about the fact that they were ill or injured. There were even those that had forgotten about me as well. What I realized from this is that illnesses healed by the power of Ki do not return. I thought, "What a wonderful world I have gained entry to!" I also realized that many of the people I had healed had felt some sort of hand feedback sensation. I was saliently reminded of the fact that everyone possesses Ki.

During these four years of my amateur period, I gained, through exhaustive practice with the power of Ki, the understanding that "Ki is existence itself." And I decided that I would continue my journeys in the world of Ki, a world that held many things unknown to me.

Discovery of the Foot Feedback Sensation

One day, while I was continuing my practice of healing through Kiryo. I was sending Ki via hand-waving to a Kiryo recipient that was laying on the floor face up. I followed the usual order: head, heart, and lower abdomen. Next, I moved to the soles of the patient's feet, and began to send Ki to them, when suddenly, I had the insight that the palms of the hands and the soles of the feet might really be one and the same. It is irrefutable that we can feel Ki with our palms. Curious whether or not this was true for the soles of our feet as well, I placed the sole of my left foot about four inches away from that of the Kiryo recipient I was treating.

Scarcely had I done so when I began to feel a faint fuzzy sensation in the sole of my left foot. I thought, "Wow! You can feel this sensation with the soles of your feet, too!" I decided to leave my foot in the same position, to see whether or not the sensation would grow stronger. It did, and I realized then that, just like the palm of the hand, the sole of the foot, too, could be used in healing. This was the discovery of the foot feedback sensation. Subsequently, the use of the sole of the foot became a fundamental part of healing in Kiryo practice: we refer to this sort of healing as "Sole Kiryo."

The Ki energy that is emitted from the sole of the foot is thought to be three times stronger than that emitted from the palm. Because Ki energy emitted from the sole of the foot sends stimulation from the Kiryo recipient's peripheral nerves to his or her central nerves, thereby causing muscular and blood flow adjustment, it is indispensable towards the improvement of one's health. However, as a trade-off, the sole of the foot is only one-third as good as the palm of the hand at perceiving bodily information.

Furthermore, when using Sole Kiryo for healing, the exchange should be sole to sole, and energy should be sent from the Kiryo practitioner's sole to that of the recipient. Kiryo should be conducted in a quiet and composed manner.

Kiryo Mastery (Exercise)

The Configurations of Kiryo Mastery Were Epochal Natural Discoveries

When and how exactly did the configurations of Kiryo Mastery (Exercise) taught at the academy come about?

The origin of the fundamental form of Kiryo was discovered while playing with the hand feedback sensation explained previously. As I was enjoying the cool, blowing feeling of the hand feedback sensation, I held a very simple, unassuming question deep within my heart: what was this sensation, and why was it occurring? This is precisely why the various configurations of Kiryo mastery developed so naturally and organically. At the time, I had no awareness of the idea of sensory exchange. I merely was interested in whether or not I could feel "something" when exposed to Ki.

Eventually, others began to be able to become aware of the presence or absence of the sensation in their palms as well. The first people for whom this happened were my parents, and it happened in their first palm exchange session. At the time, they had no awareness of the hand feedback sensation, and merely were able to say whether they "felt something" or "didn't feel anything."

My father had some trouble sensing the flow, but my mother was able to sense it almost immediately. My mother's stomach was in bad shape, and she had lost so much weight that she was barely 70 pounds. Truth be told, I happened upon other Kiryo Mastery discoveries here. That is, I realized that the ill are in such need of Ki that they are easily able to feel its flow. The other, which holds true even in the light of my experiences following the one with my parents, is that females are, in comparison to men, much more sensitive to Ki.

For some time after that, I would go to my friends and acquaintances, ask them to extend their palms, and, by asking, "can you feel this, or do you not feel anything?" I would, in a playful manner, explore the hand feedback sensation. However, at the time, these actions caused others to call me "weird," which was quite painful for me.

Alongside all this, I had also begun to practice healing itself. The effect of my Ki healing was astounding, and it was especially fast-acting on surgical ailments. And once the effects of my healing would begin to manifest, my patients would come up to me saying "Thank you so much," or "Thanks to you, my pain is gone," with smiles on their faces. These smiles were a tremendous joy to me. These smiles and the words of gratitude they accompanied are truly what led me into the world of the Kiryo of today.

Eventually, I became able to naturally conduct Ki exchange between my palms and those of people interested in Kiryo or Kiryo patients. This practice became the fundamental configuration of person-to-person, paired Ki exchange. The issue of merely asking whether my partner did or didn't feel "something" changed to a mutual eliciting and heightening of Ki itself.

Since my amateur days, I have read many books on the subject of Ki. I have also attended and participated in lectures, research seminars, experiencing the practices demonstrated therein, as well as listening to the opinions of many different individuals on the subject. Based on what I have witnessed and experienced, in other disciplines, attempts are made to come to grips with the world of Ki via such things as superhuman power, willpower, concentration, meditation, visualization, contemplation, breathing, and calisthenics. In my amateur days, I, too, attempted all of these things. For some reason, they didn't fit quite well with my preferences, and so these pursuits ended as mere attempts.

When conducting Kiryo exercise, one uses conscious orders to switch from the world of cognition to the world of sensation. They become relaxed, open, and feel as they are, allowing themselves to become mediums for the natural energy known as Ki. This unlocks mastery of Ki energy and perceptive and differentiative abilities. In the world of Kiryo, conscious thought or creativity and ingenuity are not needed. All one needs to do is heighten their hand, foot, and body feedback sensations; a world of exceedingly powerful healing waits just beyond that horizon.

Kiryo mastery is truly an epochal advancement. During the Ki exchanges with animals, detailed in Chapter 1, the animals were able to relax and lay down precisely because I cleared my mind completely of all thoughts and simply allowed myself to feel as I was.

Kiryo Mastery is Neurotransmissive Exchange

In retrospect, the discovery of the twin sensory nerves would not have been possible without the help of the students of the Kiryo Academy. If I had insisted on remaining in my own little world, this discovery would not have happened. When the students all gather in the classroom and begin to practice the configurations of Kiryo mastery, their actions bring about a series of sensory phenomena. As I attempted to define and name these various sensory phenomena, the existence of the twin sensory nerves became clear.

Though the journey started with the simple question of "what is this cool, blowing feeling I notice," because I continued to practice "feeling as I am" in accordance with the principles of what we may call Kiryo wisdom—Kiryo is openness, Kiryo is becoming a medium for natural energy—I was able to grasp the concept of Ki, which ultimately led to the discovery of the twin sensory nerves.

Kiryo mastery uses single-person exchange or one-on-one exchange to mutually awaken the twin sensory nerves, and thereby achieve neurotransmissive (Ki) exchange.

For example, in the case of single-person exchange, you hold both of your hands about four inches apart and allow your awareness to rest in your left and right palms; upon doing so, neurotransmissive exchange will begin. This is because the twin sensory nerves in your left hand and the twin sensory nerves in your right hand are awakening each other. In the case of one-on-one exchange, the twin sensory nerves in your own palms awaken those in your partner's palms. This is neurotransmissive exchange.

This neurotransmissive exchange allows for the activation of the principle of neurotransmissive flux. I have previously explained what the activity of this principle does, but because its effects are seen every time we hold mastery courses in our classrooms, let us take a closer look at them.

First, two people form a pair and sit facing each other. Each checks the other's pulse. Next, one asks his or her partner to extend both of their hands, together. Then, one holds his or her own palm about four inches away from his or her partner's palms. Upon beginning hand-waving from left to right, he or she will notice immediately that his or her partner's palms have begun to redden, and a red-and-white spotted pattern will appear. This is because the mutual awakening of the twin sensory nerves has caused blood to collect in the practitioners' palms.

If the person with one hand extended switches to their other hand and performs the hand-waving process in the same way, he or she will notice that blood will again collect in the same way. In a few words, this process is proof that stimulation of the twin sensory nerves can cause blood flow. Additionally, exercise will cause neurotransmissive exchange; when the exercise has finished, both you and your partner should re-check each other's pulse.

I have described these changes before, but you should be able to detect the following changes in your pulse. It should be composed and supple, firm, robust, and thick. The composed and supple nature of the pulse is due to the parasympathetic nerves, and the firm, robust, and thick nature of the pulse is due to the sympathetic nerves; these changes together are proof that both systems have activated.

In a few words, we can see that activation of the twin sensory nerves has improved the balance of the autonomic nervous system, vitalizing it and improving blood circulation.

As blood circulation improves, the twin sensory nerves themselves are vitalized. Vitalization of the twin sensory causes pain and pain-like sensations to leave the body through the manual feedback sensation, and one becomes able to master Ki energy and their perceptive/differentiative abilities.

Single-Person Exchange (Kiryo Mastery)

Single-person exchange (Sometimes referred to as "alone exchange.") refers to the process of becoming a medium of natural energy (heaven-earth unification energy), awakening ones' twin sensory nerves (the Kiryo nerve and the wave perception nerve) via the Ki response sensations, and thereby bringing about neurotransmissive exchange. This single-person exchange allows for the mastery of Ki energy and perceptive/differentiative ability. At the same time, it draws out healing power.

Before beginning an explanation of exercise, I would like to once again explain some fundamental concepts related to Kiryo mastery and its methods.

Additionally, perceptive and differentiative (pain and pain-like sensations) items 1 to 13 listed in the table on pages 122 and beyond have been ranked (beginner, intermediate, advanced) in accordance with the results of many years of Kiryo practice. The words of academy students and people who had their illnesses and injuries healed via Kiryo are the ones that were ranked in the aforementioned table.

Fundamental Principles of Kiryo

(1) Pain and pain-like sensations (particularly those of the palm) are completely different from illness and injury. They are senses felt by the perceptive/differentiative ability of the wave perception nerve. If one ceases placing one's awareness in one's palms, these sensations also subside.

These wonderful sensations allow for differentiation between plants, jewels, etc., and especially allow for the differentiation of when parts of the body affected by illness and injury are being healed. These sensations are what vitalize the brainstem and autonomic nerves and allow for the activation of the neurotransmissive flux principle.

(2) We often say that "seeing is believing," but in the world of Kiryo, "feeling is believing." This world can only be understood through experience and feeling. It is impossible to probe its depths with a human intellect. Above all, Kiryo is a world of sensation.

(3) As pain or pain-like sensations in the palms or soles of the feet grow stronger in response to Kiryo, one's proficiency at the

practice of Kiryo also increases. Alongside this, one's body becomes healthier, and Ki energy that can be used to heal the illnesses and injuries of others increases, and its effects become apparent. Even if you cannot feel the hand feedback sensation, every time you practice Kiryo exercise, your Ki energy is heightened, and eventually the hand feedback sensation will be strongly felt. Ki energy and perceptive/differentiative ability are two sides of the same coin.

(4) Upon beginning Kiryo exercises, the twin sensory nerves, the brainstem, and the autonomic nerves are all activated, and muscular and blood flow adjustment begins. The principle of neurotransmissive flux is activated. The hand feedback sensation, the foot feedback sensation, and the body feedback sensation all become stronger.

Mastery Methods

(1) When beginning the exercise, please place your awareness in your palms, soles, or your entire body, as is indicated in the explanation or the figure itself.

Placing your awareness in some part of your body is what allows for the switch from the world of cognition to the world of sensation. This causes the awakening of the twin sensory nerves. This is the beginning of Kiryo mastery.

(2) Once you have placed your awareness, all that is left is to feel as you are.

This "feeling as you are" is the fundamental principle of Kiryo; it is everything. It acts upon on the nerves, and it activates our physiological framework. This allows for the mastery of Ki energy and perceptive/differentiative ability, and it draws out one's innate healing ability.

(3) In Kiryo, one's nerves remain in their natural state. By placing our awareness and feeling as we are, we assume our natural state, without a single iota of cognitive activity.

83

There are those that experience involuntary movement[3] upon beginning exercise, but those people need not worry. Involuntary movement is movement that occurs independent of an individual's intention, but with regards to that individual's healing, it is a necessary movement. It is part of our physiological framework, and therefore it is not to be debated in the world of cognition whether or not it is a good or bad thing. Stopping the placement of one's awareness will immediately also stop involuntary movement. In the world of Kiryo, we refer to this involuntary movement as "healing muscle movement."

(4) Kiryo is the process of becoming a medium for natural energy.

By becoming a medium for the natural energy known as Ki, we can master Ki energy and perceptive/differentiative ability. In Kiryo, there is no need to attempt to devise creative or ingenious ways for taking in or emitting Ki. All that is needed is for one to allow oneself to feel as they are, and become a medium for natural energy.

(5) In Kiryo, we do not use things like willpower, concentration, visualization, meditation, contemplation, breathing techniques, or calisthenics.

One simply only needs to feel as they are with their palms, soles, or entire body. Eventually, they will become able to feel the manual, foot, and body feedback sensations. There is one exception: in the 11th exercise configuration, the training actually does make use of a conscious breathing technique.

(6) Kiryo exercise can be done anywhere and at any time. While talking, while watching TV, or while looking at the scenery outdoors. Do not give up; be patient and perseverant in your practice of Kiryo exercise, and your Ki energy and perceptive/differentiative ability will steadily improve.

_____

[3] For example, involuntary movement can be when one's arms or legs begin shaking during a healing session without the individual noticing.

(7) As your perceptive/differentiative abilities become more advanced, one of your hands will become your "Ki-dominant hand" and the hand feedback sensation will become stronger in it.

Kiryo healing involves using one's Ki-dominant hand to perceive and differentiate the affected parts of a person and heal them. There is no need to use both hands.

Exercise 1: Palm Gap Exchange

Relax your body and mind, hold your palms approximately four inches apart, and place your awareness in them. The twin sensory nerves in your left hand and the twin sensory nerves in your right hand will begin exchanging energy. Even if you don't feel anything, do not move your body or try to gather your concentration or consciously try to force out Ki; just feel as you are.

The truth is, the moment you place your awareness in your right and left palms, palm Ki exchange is occurring. It is just that initially, there is no hand feedback sensation, so it is difficult to tell that it is happening. If you do not remove your awareness from your palms, Ki will continue to be exchanged (refer to Illustration 1 and Table 1).

Exercise 2: Palm Ki Kneading Exchange

This time, we will move our right and left palms up and down, all the while feeling as we are. We do not move both in the same direction at the same time; instead, if we move one up, we move the other down. Doing this increases the Ki exchange sensation, and the Ki exchange sensation becomes easier to detect (refer to Illustration 2 and Table 2).

4 inches
(approx.)

(1) Palm Gap Exchange

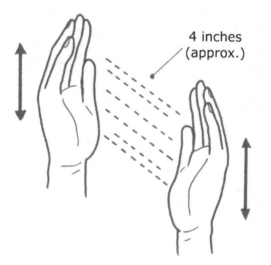

4 inches
(approx.)

(2) Palm Ki Kneading Exchange

(1) Palm Gap Exchange

Beginner	• a faint cool, blowing feeling • a warmish feeling • the feeling of wind on your hands • a faint tingly feeling • a faint expansive feeling • a faint numbness • a faint something • a fluttery feeling	• a faint hotness • a faint pressure • a faint compression • a faint feeling of being touched • a slight burning sensation • a slight prickly sensation
Intermediate	• a strong cool, blowing feeling • a hot feeling • a pain-like sensation • a light tingling feeling • an electric feeling • a pain-like electric feeling • a throbbing feeling • a smarting feeling	• an oozing feeling • a tickly feeling • a prickly sensation • an itchy sensation • a squirmy feeling • a calm feeling • a burning sensation
Advanced	• a strong painful feeling • a hot pain • a strong scorching feeling • a pinching pain • a strong electric feeling in the dominant hand • a strong pinching pain • the dominant hand hurting • the entire palm begins to feel a pinching pain	• a strong, painful burning sensation • the entire palm begins to throb and hurt • an aching pain • a strong compression and throbbing feeling • a distinct pain • the entire palm begins to hurt

(2) Palm Ki Kneading Exchange

Beginner	• a faint something • the feeling of a warm thing moving • a light numb-like feeling • a light pressure • a sensation that something is between your hands • a compressed-air feeling	• the feeling that a soft ball is between your hands • a warm feeling • the feeling of warm water • a light windy feeling • a faint stress on your palms • the feeling of being touched • an expansive feeling
Intermediate	• palms being magnetically drawn to each other • a light tingling feeling • a light pain • the feeling of a heavy burden being lifted • a strong pressure • a prickly feeling	• the feeling of being slightly pulled • a slightly painful, electric feeling • a staticky electric feeling • the feeling of a soft thread entwining your palms
Advanced	• the center of your palm grows hot and hurts • your palms begin to tingle electrically (esp. dominant hand) • a strong pain felt in your palms • your Ki-dominant hand begins to hurt • electric pain becomes stronger	• your entire palm feels a strong, pinching pain • a prickly feeling and strong pain • the pinching feeling of strong pain

Exercise 3: Palm-Finger Exchange

Place your hands near each other just as you did in Exercise 1, and place your awareness in your hands. Point the fingers of your left hand at the palm of your right hand. Move them slowly, almost as if raising them up, ensuring that all the while you are allowing them to feel as they are. Your right palm will also begin to feel as it is, just like your left fingers.

Continue the exercise, switching the orientation of your left and right hands periodically. This exercise will help you determine which of your hands is your Ki-dominant hand (refer to Illustration 3 and Table 3).

Exercise 4: Palm Opening and Closing Exchange

Next, we will try opening and closing our palms. In doing this, one will notice that when we move our hands apart, a pulling (connected) sensation will be felt. It is a strange feeling, almost as if the nerves of your palm are stretching and being pulled out.

First, we begin with the usual four-inch gap between our palms, allow ourselves to feel the Ki exchange sensation as we are, and then, maintaining this feeling as we are state, we slowly widen the gap between our palms.

Once we have become able to widen the gap between palms until they are our shoulder width apart, we will add in the element of up and down movement as well. If this proves difficult to do, it is okay to only move one hand up and down while widening the gap between them. Doing this will help the hand feedback sensation become easier to discern. Over time, we slowly and gradually widen the gap between our hands.

When one begins to close the gap, they will notice that they feel a pressure (compression) sensation. Also, when doing open and closing exchange, a warm, cool, blowing, and/or a tingly feeling may all be felt (refer to Illustration 4 and Table 4).

(3) Palm-Finger Exchange

(4) Palm Opening and Closing Exchange

(3) Palm-Finger Exchange

Beginner	• the feeling of being lightly tickled • the feeling of being stroked • the feeling of wind flowing • the feeling of something warm moving • the feeling of wind slipping through your fingers • the feeling of your fingers moving	
Intermediate	• a light pain • the feeling of something pulled out of your palm, through the back of the hand and into the shoulder • the strong feeling of your fingers moving • palms tingling	• fingers feel prickly • slight electric pain • a pain in the center of your palm
Advanced	• a stabbing pain in the left hand • pain alongside the strong feeling of your fingers moving • strong prickling in palms • strong tingling in palms • a distinct, strong pain • a strong electric pain	• a stabbing pain in the bones of the palm

(4) Palm Opening and Closing Exchange

Beginner	• a light pressure • a faint something • a widening and shivering feeling • a light pulling feeling • a warm pulling feeling	
Intermediate	• the feeling intensifies the farther apart you pull your hands • a feeling of being enveloped such that your hands are moving in unison • being able to feel the sensation more when widening the gap • waves echoing in the other hand • feeling gets stronger when widening past shoulder width	• the sensation changes based on the distance between the hands • a light pulling feeling • the feeling of your palms being sucked towards each other
Advanced	• a feeling like pulling a string of melted cheese • a strong pain • a pain, alongside the feeling of pulling a thread of silk • a strong pain that feels like pulling an accordion	

Applied Exercises for Feeling Ki

Once we have mastered the basic exercises, we will try inserting something between our palms and pairing our palms with something else other than each other and performing energy exchange. The many configurations of single-person exchange exercise are also nothing but the healing of oneself through self-Kiryo.

Initially, the Ki power may be quite low, but continue to feel as you are and practice the exercise. It will serve as self-Kiryo. It will also serve as practice in detecting with your palm the waves of change in your body caused by the exercise itself; please try and practice it as much as you can.

Exercise 5: Palm Trans-Desk Exchange

Now that we've grown accustomed to the Ki exchange sensation, let us try placing our left and right palms above and underneath a desk, separating them by about four inches, and allowing exchange to take place as before. You should be able to perceive through this that Ki is able to pass through solid objects.

If you are able to widen the gap between your palms while keeping the desk between them, try moving your hands just as you did in Exercises 2 and 3. Slowly widen the gap between your hands, and add various different movements as needed, making sure all the while to feel as you are (refer to Illustration 5 and Table 5).

(5) Palm Trans-Desk Exchange

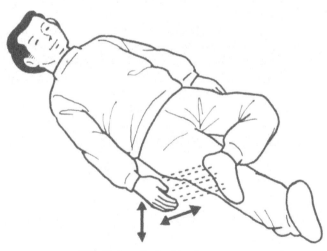

(6) Palm-Sole Exchange

94

(5) Palm Trans-Desk Exchange

Beginner	• a faint something • the feeling of something heavy • a light pulling sensation • a light pressure
Intermediate	• Ki-dominant hand feels strong, and the other weak • The center of your palm experiences an astonishing feeling • Warmth and prickliness • Cannot tell there is a desk between your hands • A strong feeling of being pulled • A slightly painful prickly feeling
Advanced	• A burning feeling in the Ki-dominant hand • A strong pain in the Ki-dominant hand • Feeling as if there isn't anything between your palms

Exercise 6: Palm-Sole Exchange

Up till now, we have been experiencing the Ki exchange sensation with the palms of our hands, but now, let us try experiencing a Ki exchange sensation of a different sort.

Lie down and extend your right leg, and place your left leg on top of it. Bend your left leg as if you are sitting cross-legged. Take your right palm and place it near the sole of your left foot, leaving a small gap between the two, and allow yourself to feel as you are, thereby beginning Ki exchange. You should be able to notice a Ki exchange sensation happening between the sole of your foot and your hand.

Once you have finished practicing that exchange, switch the configuration of your legs so that you can carry out Ki exchange with your left palm and right sole. If this is easier for you to do seated rather than lying down, feel free to do the practice seated (refer to Illustration 6 and Table 6).

Exercise 7: Sole Gap Exchange

Lie down, point the soles of your feet towards each other, and form a small gap between them. Allow your hands to rest. Place your awareness in your right and left soles, and allow them to feel as they are, and perform Ki exchange.

If this is easier for you to do seated than lying down, feel free to do it seated (refer to Illustration 7 and Table 7).

(6) Palm-Sole Exchange

Beginner	• a faint something • a light tingling in the sole of your foot • a slight sensation in your palm • a lack of sensation in your foot	
Intermediate	• Feeling a pulling sensation predominantly in the hand; the legs tingle • Palms feel a heavy pain • Able to feel more sensation in your palms • Your hands tingle and your feet become hot	• Warmth in the palms and prickling in the soles • Palms throb and feel heavy • Electric feeling in palms • Electric feeling in soles • Hands and feet feel electric, feet are also tickly
Advanced	• Feel it strongly in the back of the hand • The Ki-dominant hand and foot strongly and freely feel the sensation • Pain in the soles of the feet • A dull, burning pain in the soles of the feet	

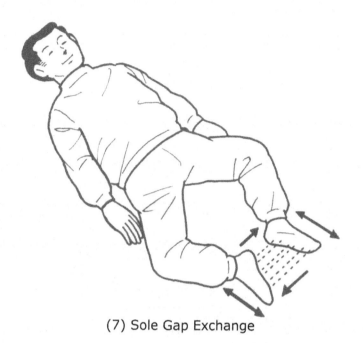

(7) Sole Gap Exchange

(8) Palm-Abdominal Exchange

(7) Sole Gap Exchange

Beginner	• A light tingling sensation • A faint something • Only sense something upon being told of it • Don't feel anything	
Intermediate	• The feeling that something is coming out of your soles • A heavy sensation that won't let up unless you move your feet • Both legs tingling • The soles grow warm and the whole body heats up	• Soles of your feet throb • An electric tingling in the soles of your feet
Advanced	• Clearly feel the sensation, and can make it move around at will • A strong electric tingling • A burning pain • A cold, airy pain in both soles	

(8) Palm-Abdominal Exchange

Beginner	<ul><li>A faint something</li><li>Something crawling on top of your belly</li><li>Definitely able to feel something but only very faintly</li><li>Somewhat able to feel something</li></ul>	
Intermediate	<ul><li>Lower abdomen suddenly becomes hot</li><li>A heavy, sinking pain</li><li>A ringing feeling as if the lower abdomen has become numb</li><li>Able to feel the movement of one's palms</li></ul>	<ul><li>Feeling as if you're being lifted up and pressed down in accordance with your hands' up and down movements</li><li>Able to feel one's pulse</li><li>Legs feel electric</li></ul>
Advanced	<ul><li>The feeling that one's whole body is moving</li><li>Your intestine moves</li><li>Able to feel something originate in your lower abdomen and move to the rest of your body</li><li>Strongly able to feel your hands moving in all directions</li></ul>	

Exercise 8: Palm-Abdomen Exchange

Lie down again, and place your palm slightly above your lower abdomen. Allow yourself to feel the Ki exchange sensation in your palm and your lower abdomen as you are. Ki exchange will occur between your palm and your lower abdomen. In the event that you cannot really discern the sensation, move your palm up and down and left to right.

Once you've finished the exercise with one hand, switch to the other (refer to Illustration 8 and Table 8).

Exercise 9: Palm-Chest Exchange

This time, assume a seated position. Relax your entire body, and place your palm over your heart, about four inches away from your chest, and allow Ki exchange to begin. Allow your awareness to rest first in your hand and then your chest, feeling as you are all the while.

You should be able to feel the Ki exchange sensation. In the event that you cannot really discern the sensation, move your palm up and down. Once you've finished the exercise with one hand, switch to the other (refer to Illustration 9 and Table 9).

Exercise 10: Palm-Crown Exchange

Let us try sending Ki into the center-point of Kiryo itself: the brainstem.

In a relaxed state, lie down, and place one palm above your head, with your palm facing the crown of your skull, and begin to send Ki into your head. While doing this, place your awareness in your palm, and allow the rest of your body to go limp.

In a calm, composed manner, feel as you are, and continue to send Ki into your head. You should feel the sensation of Ki exchanging throughout your body. Once finished, do the same with your other hand (refer to Illustration 10 and Table 10).

(9) Palm-Chest Exchange

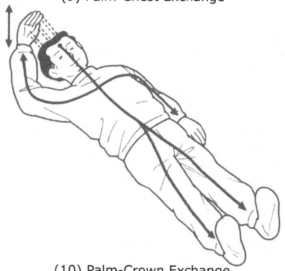

(10) Palm-Crown Exchange

(9) Palm-Chest Exchange

Beginner	• Feeling movement and a sort-of warm thing • A faint something • Chest feels warm • A light pattering in the chest • A faint feeling of being touched • Somewhat able feel something
Intermediate	• A tingling, and a thumping of the heart • A thumping sort of movement • The side of the body with the heart feels it stronger • The heart beats faster
Advanced	• Easily able to feel the movements of the hand in the chest • Moving your hand feels like passing a roller over the chest • Pain that moves along the chest with the hand

(10) Palm-Crown Exchange

Beginner	• A faint something • A faint numbness in the soles of the feet • A weak Ki-flow sensation	
Intermediate	• The feet grow warm and the palms shimmer • The face gets hot and the soles of the feet experience an oozing feeling • Head begins to spin • Soles of the feet get prickly	• The spine gets warm and the soles feel wind blowing over them • The feet feel electric • Waves beating from head to toe with one's pulse • A rumbling stomach
Advanced	• Ki-dominant pains and the feet feel scorched • Suddenly feel the sensation echo in both feet • Feeling waves throughout the whole body • Pain lances through the whole body periodically	

Exercise 11: Respiratory Whole-Body Awareness Exchange

Next, let us experience the Ki exchange sensation with our whole body.

Lie down, and imagine that as you inhale, Ki is traveling from your feet, through your body's nerves, and up to your head. When exhaling, allow that Ki to go from your head back down to your feet. In order to sense the movement of Ki, we must also allow our awareness to travel up and down our bodies, in accordance with our breathing. You should be able to feel the Ki passing through your nerves, almost like wind blowing through your body.

In the event that it is difficult for you to discern the movement of Ki through your body, you may want to try performing hand-waving corresponding to the movement of the Ki itself (refer to Illustration 11 and Table 11).

Exercise 12: Whole-Body Awareness Movement Exchange

Relax your body, place your awareness, and, feeling as you are, move your awareness of Ki around your body, reaching every nook and cranny. You may do this standing, lying down, or even sitting.

First, place your awareness in your head, followed by, in order, your shoulders, hands, chest, lower abdomen, knees, and then feet. Continue moving your awareness throughout your body, noticing the sensation of Ki flowing along with it. You should be able to discern that the sensation differs with the area in which your awareness is resting (refer to Illustration 12, Table 12).

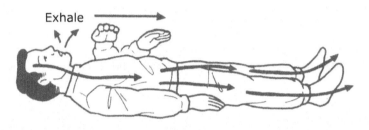

(11): Respiratory Whole-Body Awareness Exchange

(11) Respiratory Whole-Body Awareness Exchange

Beginner	<ul><li>A faint something</li><li>Faintly able to feel the movement of your five fingers</li><li>When exhaling, a light prickling</li></ul>	
Intermediate	<ul><li>When exhaling, the feeling of a warm something coming out of the hands and feet</li><li>A hot sensation exiting the hands and feet</li><li>The feeling of a hot something passing through the inside of your body, towards the feet</li><li>When exhaling, an electric sensation exiting the hands and feet</li></ul>	<ul><li>Wind entering the hands and feet and a warm wind exiting</li><li>With the breath, a feeling of the entire body moving at once</li><li>Hands and feet feeling electric</li><li>With the breath, an oozing feeling across the entire body</li></ul>
Advanced	<ul><li>The feeling of something strongly exiting the entire body</li><li>A strong pain moving around the body with the breath</li><li>The feeling of air entering and exiting the body</li><li>When inhaling, the feeling of your body swelling up</li><li>When exhaling, the feeling of air draining out of the entire body</li></ul>	

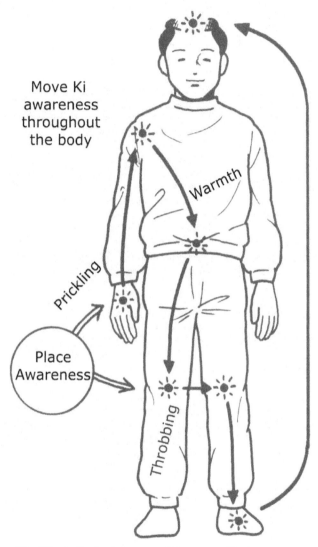

(12): Whole-Body Awareness Movement Exchange

(12) Whole-Body Awareness Movement Exchange

Beginner	• A faint something • A hot tingling in the hands and feet, and a warmth in the chest • The faint feeling that something is moving • A slight electric feeling • Somewhat capable of feeling one's awareness moving around
Intermediate	• Each part feels hot and tingly • The muscles move • The part feels warm, and you can feel blood moving through it • The heart throbs and then feels electric
Advanced	• The chest and heart hurt strongly • The movement of one's awareness causes every corner of the body to react • Strongly feeling the entire process throughout the body, with pain lancing through each part in turn

Kiryo Exercise using Objects

Up till now, we have been performing Kiryo exercise using only our own bodies. Now, we will employ objects to practice exchanging Ki with things outside our bodies. Ki is a natural energy: it resides in all things, and all things possess Ki. Thus, we can exchange Ki with things we find in nature.

However, not all things emit Ki to the same degree. There are some whose emissions are hard to detect. Accordingly, I have recommended here only objects which emit Ki especially strongly. These should also be things you already possess; use them to try these exercises.

Exercise 13: Palm-Jewel and Palm-Plant Exchange

Stones strongly emit Ki. That being said, a random stone off the ground is unlikely to emit any particularly strong amount of Ki.

Take a jewel from some of your jewelry, or, if you have it, a power stone (crystals, lapis lazuli, rose quartz, and other such wave-redolent natural stones) and place it on a desk. We will now send Ki from above into this stone.

If you are using a jewel, diamonds and amethysts emit particularly strong Ki.

Place your awareness in your hands and continue the exchange for some time. The Ki (waves) of the stone should be transmitted into your hands. If you are having trouble detecting the flow of Ki, perform hand-waving, taking care not to touch the stone.

Jewels and power stones, depending on their specific qualities, emit hard, soft, round, sharp, and all other sorts of differently-natured Ki. Once you are able to clearly discern the nature of the Ki of your specific stone, stand up while continuing to send Ki into it, and increase the distance between you and the stone. Some are able to feel the stone's Ki even several meters away.

Next, we will be exchanging Ki with plants; these can include potted plants, or the flowers in your garden.

Place your awareness in your hands, and, feeling as you are, perform Ki exchange with the plant. You may use both hands at once, or one at a time. Performing hand-waving will help you discern the Ki exchange better. Each plant's Ki (wave) nature will be slightly different, so I advise that you try exchanging with several different plants. If you happen to have a large tree near you, try exchanging with it as well.

When exchanging with a large plant, it can be quite difficult to place one's hands above it to send Ki downwards. In such situations, stand in front of the plant, raise both hands, and look up. Perform the exchange in this position. Just like with large trees, you will be able to feel a stronger Ki emitted from plants that are older (see Illustration 13 and Table 13).

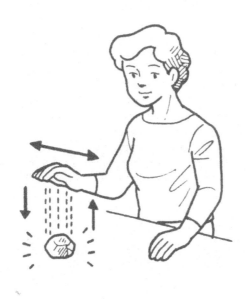

(13) Palm-Jewel and Palm-Plant Exchange

112

(13) Palm-Jewel and Palm-Plant Exchange

Beginner	• A tingling in the palms • A faint something • A warm, heavy feeling	• A light, fluffy feeling • A light numbness • Unable to perceive anything • A light chill
Intermediate	• The crystal feels cold, and the tree feels thick and linear • Warmth and pressure • The reaction of the crystal sphere is quite strong • Numbness • Tingling	• An electric feeling • A different feeling for each stone • Different feeling for each plant
Advanced	• Strongly feel both the stone and tree, and each feels different • The center of the palm feels pain, and the fingers feel electric • Able to discern the difference in each thing's waveforms • Truly able to properly feel the sensation, and perceive it as well	• A strongly electric feeling • Each stone has a strong waveform, and the pain is unbearable • Easily able to discern the difference in each tree's waveform

Person-to-Person Exchange

Person-to-Person Exchange refers to Ki exchange between two people that involves both becoming a medium for natural energy (heaven-earth unification energy) and awakening each other's twin sensory nerves (Kiryo nerve and the waveform perception nerve) via the Kiryo sensation. This person-to-person exchange enables one to master the perception and differentiation of Ki energy, as well as the drawing-out of each person's healing power.

Person-to-person exchange, depending on the specific configuration of Kiryo mastery being employed, can be performed with no limit on the number of participants. The more people that are participating together in the exercise, the greater the energy that will be accumulated, and the greater the relaxation space that will be created. A large number of people together awakening each other's twin sensory nerves through Ki exchange gives rise to a very great power indeed.

The relaxation space—that is, the healing space—that is created as a result of the person-to-person exchange of multiple people is itself the Kiryo space that draws out and heightens the Ki energy perception and differentiation ability of each participant. Additionally, person-to-person exchange is a form of preventative Kiryo (health maintenance), a sort of Kiryo that stops illnesses before they can even occur. Of course, those who are already ill can use the power of Ki to recover their health.

Next, I would like to explain some fundamental points of Kiryo mastery (exercise).

Hand Feedback Exchange, Foot Feedback Exchange, & Body Feedback Exchange

Hand-feedback exchange, which uses the palm of the hand, foot-feedback exchange, which uses the sole of the foot, and body-feedback exchange, which uses the whole body, are Ki exchange techniques that cause mutual awakening of the twin sensory nerves. They also lead to mastery of the feedback sensations.

Hand-feedback exchange helps one master the hand-feedback sensation; foot-feedback exchange, the foot-feedback sensation; body-feedback exchange, the body-feedback sensation.

There is a certain order to the mastery of these three sensations. First, one must learn hand feedback exchange, then foot feedback exchange, and finally body feedback exchange. I have ranked these sensations in the following table.

Table 3: Mastery of the Sensations

Hand Feedback Sensation	Foot Feedback Sensation	Body Feedback Sensation
Beginner		
Intermediate	Beginner	
Advanced	Intermediate	Beginner

One begins with the hand feedback sensation. When your ability in the hand feedback sensation reaches an intermediate level, one's ability with the foot feedback sensation will be at a beginner level. And when hand feedback sensation ability is at an advanced level, foot feedback sensation ability will be at an intermediate level, and body feedback sensation ability will be at a beginner level. This is the natural order of mastery that occurs as one acquires these sensations by feeling as they are. The physiological makeup that all of us possess is what causes this flow, this progression.

The hand feedback sensation is the foundation of Kiryo mastery. As your hand feedback sensation strengthens, your Ki energy also grows stronger. And once you achieve a certain level, your Ki energy ability and your perceptive and differentiative abilities become two sides of the same coin. Activation of the principle of neurotransmissive flux causes these abilities to grow and improve. They cannot disappear, and you will never lose them.

Sender, Receiver, and Reciprocal Sending Defined (Mutual Awakening of the Twin Sensory Nerves)

The Sender: The person who, by moving their hands, feet, or body, amplifies their exchange sensation.

The Receiver: The person who, by feeling as they are the hand, foot, or body movements of the sender, amplifies their exchange sensation.

Reciprocal Sending: Occurs when both participants play the role of sender and actively exchange Ki with each other.

The Basic Ki Exchange Sensations

The Ki exchange sensation is brought about by the mutual awakening of the twin sensory nerves as caused by drawing out and mutual amplification of both Ki energy and one's perceptive and differentiative ability.

Differences in the specific movements of the sender give rise to different Ki exchange sensations. Here, I will use the hand feedback sensation to explain the various types of sensations that exist.

1) Still Exchange Sensation

The sender and receiver exchange Ki while remaining still. For example, during two-person palm exchange, the receiver extends both of his or her hands, palms facing up. The sender holds his or her hands about four inches above those of the receiver, palms facing down. One will notice that the Ki exchange sensation in their palms grows stronger.

2) Ki Kneading Sensation

This is the sensation felt when one uses hand-waving to massage the Ki being exchanged.

The sender, or both senders in reciprocal sending, kneads the Ki that is being exchanged. Kneading causes both Ki energy and perceptive and differentiative ability to be drawn out and amplified.

3) Pulling Sensation (Connected Sensation)

When the sender kneads Ki above the palms of the receiver and then pulls their hands away from those of the receiver, both parties will feel a pulling sensation, or a connected sensation.

People whose hand feedback sensation has progressed to a certain level may try standing up as they draw their hands away from those of their partner; this will increase the pulling sensation. The further you go, the stronger the sensation.

This may be due to the fact that Ki exchange spaces possess some quality that allows them to amplify energy.

4) Pressure Sensation (Compression Sensation)

As the palms of the sender, which start out some distance away from those of the receiver, approach those of the receiver, a pressure or compression sensation is increasingly strongly felt. This pressure sensation/compression sensation is one of the exchange sensations that inform us of the existence of Ki energy.

5) Coming and Going Sensation

The sender kneads the Ki with the palms of the receiver. As the sender waves his or her hands from left to right, and then from right to left, the receiver should feel a sense of coming (as the sender's hands approach their own) and going (as the sender's hands move away). This exchange sensation is known as the coming and going sensation.

6) Ki-Throwing Sensation

This refers to the exchange sensation felt when a sender faces one or more receivers and uses their Ki-dominant hand to "throw" Ki towards them.

If the sender keeps their hand still after throwing the Ki, they will be able to feel a strong Ki exchange with the receiver. In addition, the receiver should feel a strong Ki exchange after receiving the Ki thrown by the sender.

7) Ki-Hitting Sensation

This exercise is to be done with multiple people. The sensation is felt when the sender points their Ki-dominant palm towards the floor, and makes three hitting motions without actually touching the floor.

The first time and the second time should be small, light motions. On the third time, the sender should make a hard, exaggerated hitting motion and then still their hand. The exchange sensation will be transmitted to the receiver, and if he or she waits for some time, the sensation will grow stronger. The receiver may also directly receive the hitting exchange, and the sensation will strengthen in the same way.

Kiryo Mastery: Type A, Type B, and Type C

We consider the sender to be the centerpoint of the exercises. Receivers respond to the movements of the senders and so maintain the Ki exchange.

Depending on the proportion of senders to receivers participating, any given exercise can be further subdivided into one of three types. To make things simple, let us assume that there are 10 people in the group we are considering.

Type A exercise is one against many. For our group of ten people, one would play the role of sender, and the remaining nine would be receivers.

Type B exercise is many against many. For our group of ten people, we could have two senders and eight receivers, or five senders and five receivers, or any similar arrangement.

Type C exercise is many against one. One person will be receiver, and the remaining nine members of our group will all be senders.

During person-to-person exchange, we combine the following elements when pursuing the mastery of Kiryo: senders and receivers; hand feedback, foot feedback, and body feedback exchange; Ki exchange sensations; configurations; and Types A , B, and C.

Next, I will explain the emblematic configurations of Kiryo mastery exercise. Because Kiryo mastery is a world of "feeling as you are," we will use the exchange sensations I have described up till now as a foundation for this explanation.

Two-Person Exercises

Palm to Palm Exchange

Palm to palm exchange is the most basic configuration for mastering the hand feedback sensation. This holds true not only for single person exercises but also for two-person exercises.

This is always the first configuration that we perform during Kiryo mastery courses at the Academy.

Illustration 1 (See illustrations on following page)

- Hand Feedback Exchange (Hand Feedback Sensation)
- Sender on right, receiver on left
- Sender and receiver hold their palms still and use them to perceive and differentiate the Ki exchange sensation.
- Sender uses their palms to perform Ki kneading five to six times above the palms of the receiver.
- Receiver perceives and differentiates the sender's Ki kneading.

Illustration 2

- Hand Feedback Exchange (Hand Feedback Sensation)
- Sender on right, receiver on left
- Sender raises their palms upwards and perceives and differentiates the pulling or connected sensation.
- Sender lowers their palms back towards those of the receiver and perceives and differentiates the pressure or compression sensation.
- Receiver remains in a "feel as they are" state while perceiving and differentiating the movements of the palms of the sender. Receiver should, like the sender, perceive and differentiate the pulling/connecting and pressure/compression sensations of the exchange.

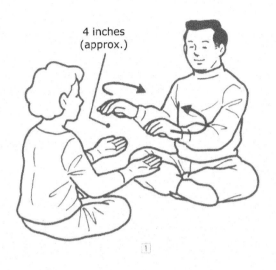

4 inches
(approx.)

Illustration 1 and 2

121

Illustration 3

- Hand Feedback Exchange (Hand Feedback Sensation)
- Sender on right, receiver on left
- Sender kneads Ki by drawing circles with their hands from outside to inside. Perform this action near the palms of the receiver 5 - 6 times, then farther above them 5 - 6 more times.
- Receiver should perceive and differentiate the Ki kneading of the palms of the sender.

Illustration 3

Sole to Sole Exchange

Sole to sole exchange is the most basic configuration for mastering the foot feedback sensation. While performing Kiryo,

I believe we should always make use of our feet. The Ki energy of the soles is about three times stronger than that of the palms.

Illustration 4

- Foot Feedback Exchange (Foot Feedback Sensation)
- Sender on the right, receiver on the left
- Sender and receiver hold their soles still and use them to perceive and differentiate the Ki exchange sensation

Illustration 5

- Foot Feedback Exchange (Foot Feedback Sensation)
- Sender on the right, receiver on the left
- Sender holds their sole about four inches away from the sole of the receiver. Sender moves their sole in a circle 5 – 6 times, keeping it parallel with the sole of the receiver
- Receiver perceives and differentiates the kneading of Ki of the sender's sole

4 inches
(approx.)

Illustration 4 and 5
124

Illustration 6

- Foot Feedback Exchange (Foot Feedback Sensation)
- Sender moves their right foot to the right to perceive and differentiate the pulling or connected sensation
- Sender returns their right foot to the original position, perceiving and differentiating the pressure or compression sensation
- Receiver remains in a "feel as they are" state while perceiving and differentiating the movements of the sole of the sender. Receiver should, like the sender, perceive and differentiate the pulling/connecting and pressure/compression sensations of the exchange.
- Switch to the left feet and perform the exercise once more.

During two-person exercises like Palm-to-Palm Exchange and Sole-to-Sole Exchange, both participants can play the role of sender at once.

Please examine the following table, which lists Kiryo mastery configurations for two-person exercise. We practice all of these exercises regularly in the mastery courses at the Academy (refer to Table 4).

Illustration 6

Two-Person Exercises

Palm to Palm Exchange
- with both sitting down
- with sender standing up

Fingertips Exchange
Fingertips to Palm Exchange
Palm to Sole Exchange
Sole to Sole Exchange
Separated Exchange
Two-Person Building Exchange
Ki-Throwing exchange

Ki-Kicking exchange
Folded Hands Exchange
Intertwined Hands Exchange
Finger-Pin Exchange
Hand Clapping Gap Exchange
Hand-Foot Clapping Gap Exchange
Push Out Exchange
Coming and Going Exchange
Body Feedback Exchange
Human Battery Exchange

Multi-Person Exercises

Cosmos Palm Exchange

Cosmos Palm Exchange is among the most exemplary of the multiple-person exercises. It is a form of hand feedback exchange, and both senders and receivers can use it to master the hand feedback sensation.

The group sits in a circle, with the receivers extending both of their hands towards the center; the arrangement evokes the petals of the cosmos flower, which is why I named the exercise Cosmos Palm Exchange.

People of all skill levels, from beginner to advanced, can participate in this easily understood hand feedback exchange exercise. It creates collective energy and a relaxation space.

Illustration 7

- Hand Feedback Exchange (Hand Feedback Sensation)
- There is one sender. The six receivers sit in a circle facing the sender, and extend their hands, palms up, towards its center.
- As shown in (1), the sender situates themselves in the middle of the circle, palms facing down. Keeping their hand still in a position about four inches above the level of the hands of the receivers, the sender will perceive and differentiate Ki exchange with the six receivers. The sender then slowly draws three circles in the air to perform Ki kneading.
- Next, as shown by (2), the sender slowly and smoothly makes two laps around the circle, keeping their hand four

inches above those of the receivers. After passing by each receiver twice, the sender returns to the center of the circle.

- The six receivers should remain in a "feel as you are" state and perceive and differentiate the movements of the palm of the sender. In (1), they will perceive and differentiate the Ki-kneading Sensation, and in (2), the coming and going sensation.

Illustration 8

- Hand Feedback Exchange (Hand Feedback Sensation)
- There is one sender. The six receivers sit in a circle facing the sender, and extend their hands, palms up, towards its center.
- The sender rises to their feet, bringing their hand up with them as they do so. The sender should perceive and differentiate the pulling or connected sensation. With their hand still raised, the sender then draws three large circles in midair to perform Ki kneading.
- The sender then lowers their hand back to its original position by bending at the waist and lowering their arm. They should perceive and differentiate the pressure or compression sensation.
- The six receivers should remain in a "feel as you are" state as they use their palms to perceive and differentiate the movements of the palms of the sender. The receivers should also, like the sender, perceive and differentiate the pulling or connected sensation, the Ki-kneading sensation, and the pressure or compression sensation.

Illustration 7

Illustration 8

130

Illustration 9

- Hand Feedback Exchange (Hand Feedback Sensation)
- The sender will place their hand in a position about four inches above the floor, with their palm facing down. They will perform a Ki-hitting motion three times. They will then hold their palm still, and perceive and differentiate the Ki exchange sensation that will be growing stronger between themselves and the six receivers.
- The six receivers should perceive and differentiate the three Ki-hitting sensations as caused by the sender. Then, as the sender did, they should perceive and differentiate the Ki exchange sensation that will be growing stronger between themselves and the sender.

Illustration 9

Wagon Wheel Exchange

Of the multiple-person exercises, Wagon Wheel Exchange is one of the configurations most exemplary of the foot feedback sensation. Here, the sender uses hand feedback exchange and the receivers use foot feedback exchange. As the arrangement of the receivers sitting in circle with their legs extended towards the center reminds me of the spokes of a wagon wheel, I named this exercise Wagon Wheel Exchange.

In this configuration, the sender draws out their own hand feedback sensation by using their palm to exchange Ki with the strongly Ki-emitting soles of the receivers that surround them. The soles' ability to sense Ki is much weaker than the palms', but this exercise amplifies the Foot Feedback Sensation.

Illustration 10

- Hand Feedback Exchange (Hand Feedback Sensation) and Foot Feedback Exchange (Foot Feedback Sensation)
- There is one sender and six receivers. The receivers should face the sender and sit in a circle, extending their legs to its center.
- As in (1), the sender should hold their palm face down four inches above the floor, and, while keeping it still, perceive and differentiate Ki exchanges with soles of the receivers. The sender then slowly draws three circles in the air to perform Ki kneading.
- Next, as shown by (2), the sender slowly and smoothly makes two laps around the circle, keeping their hand four inches above the toes of the receivers. After passing by each receiver twice, the sender returns to the center of the circle.
- The six receivers should remain in a "feel as you are" state and perceive and differentiate the movements of the palm of the sender. In (1), they will perceive and differentiate the Ki-kneading sensation as produced by the sender, and

in (2), the coming and going sensation as produced by the sender.

Illustration 10

Illustration 11

- Hand Feedback Exchange (Hand Feedback Sensation)
- There is one sender. The six receivers sit in a circle facing the sender and extend their legs towards its center.
- The sender rises to their feet, bringing their hand up with them as they do so. The sender should perceive and differentiate the pulling or connected sensation. With their hand still raised, the sender then draws three large circles in midair to perform Ki kneading.
- The sender then lowers their hand back to its original position by bending at the waist and lowering their arm. They should perceive and differentiate the pressure or compression sensation.
- The six receivers should remain in a "feel as you are" state as they use their soles to perceive and differentiate the movements of the palms of the sender. The receivers should also, like the sender, perceive and differentiate the pulling or connected sensation, the Ki-kneading sensation, and the pressure or compression sensation.

Illustration 11

Illustration 12

- Hand Feedback Exchange (Hand Feedback Sensation) and Foot Feedback Exchange (Foot Feedback Sensation)
- The sender places their hand in a position about four inches above the floor, with their palm facing down. They then perform a Ki-hitting motion three times. Then they hold their palm still, and perceive and differentiate the Ki exchange sensation that will be growing stronger between themselves and the soles of the six receivers.
- The six receivers should perceive and differentiate the three Ki-hitting sensations as caused by the sender. Then, as the sender did, they should perceive and differentiate the Ki exchange sensation that will be growing stronger between themselves and the palm of the sender.

Please examine the following table, which lists Kiryo mastery configurations for multiple-person exercises. We practice all of these exercises regularly during the mastery courses at the Academy. These exercises can be done by any number of people greater than three (refer to Table 5).

Illustration 12

139

Table 5: Kiryo Mastery (Exercise) Configurations

Type A: One vs. Many
Type B: Many vs. Many
Type C: Many vs. One

Sender: Active Exchange
Receiver: Passive Exchange

Objectives

Drawing out Ki energy // Drawing out perceptive & differentiative ability
Amplifying Ki energy // Amplifying perceptive & differentiative ability
Preventative Kiryo (health management) // Health restoration through Ki energy (natural healing)

Exchange Type: Multiple-Person Exchanges

Names of Kiryo Mastery Configurations

Hand Feedback Sensation

Fingertip — Type A, B, C	Ki-Throwing — Type A, B, C	Ki-Kicking — Type A, B, C	Torus Push Out — Type A, B, C
Folded Hands — Type A, B, C	Hand Clapping Gap — Type A, B, C	Face-Up Row — Type A, B	**Building Exchanges:**
Wagon Wheel — Type A, B	Circle Hand Clapping Gap — Type A, B, C	Push Out — Type A, B, C	Three-Person Building Exchange
Torus — Type A, B, C	Hand-Foot Clapping Gap — Type A, B, C	**Gap Transmission Exchanges:**	Four-Person Building Exchange
Finger-Pin — Type A, B, C	Circle Hand-Foot Clapping Gap — Type A, B, C	Palm Gap Transmission — Type A, B	Five-Person Building Exchange
		Sole Gap Transmission — Type A, B	Linked Building Exchange

Foot Feedback Sensation

Cosmos Exchanges:	**Column Exchanges:**	**Fan Exchanges:**	**Heaven-Earth Unification Exchanges:**
Cosmos Palm — Type A, B, C	Column Palm — Type A, B, C	Fan Palm — Type A, B, C	Circle — Type A, B, C
Cosmos Fingertip — Type A, B, C	Column Fingertip — Type A, B, C	Fan Fingertip — Type A, B, C	Remote — Type A, B, C
Body Feedback — Type A, B, C	Column Sole — Type A, B, C	Fan Sole	Sunflower
	Body Column — Type A, B, C	Fan Two-Stage	Human Battery
		One-Character	
		Ten-Character	

Body Feedback Sensation	Ki is existence itself. Ki is shared by all. Heaven-earth unification energy (natural energy)

Mastery of Ki Energy and Perceptive & Differentiative Ability

Improving Ki Energy and Perceptive & Differentiative Ability

As I have mentioned, once one uses Kiryo mastery to draw out Ki energy and perception and differentiation ability, these abilities do not go away. This concept is important enough that I would like to explain it from the perspective of nervous function.

Ki exchange is the same as neurotransmissive exchange. The awakening of the twin sensory nerves causes activation of the principle of neurotransmissive flux. Once the principle of neurotransmissive flux is activated, it continues to become more and more active. Once it reaches a certain level, even if you don't practice exercises for a long time, it does not wilt or wither. In fact, it gets stronger.

Once the flux principle activates the brainstem's homeostatic power, the brainstem begins to continuously transmit strong orders. The twin sensory nerves and the autonomic nerves receive these orders and become more and more vitalized. One of the twin sensory nerves is the Kiryo nerve, which is the source of Ki energy. The other sensory nerve is the source of perceptive and differentiative ability. Thus, once one has mastered Ki energy and perceptive and differentiative ability through Kiryo mastery (exercise), these abilities will not fade or go away. In fact, they will only continue to improve.

Ki energy can heal the illnesses of others, and it can heal one's own illnesses and injuries. This healing is a very natural thing in the world of Kiryo. Because everyone possesses Ki, anyone can master it. Ki is existence itself. To live is to be Ki. Only the strength of Ki differs from person to person. All we need do is practice, day after day, the Kiryo mastery configurations.

The other ability, perceptive and differentiative ability, is the ability to perceive and differentiate various sorts of waves. This ability enables us, when healing someone, to know where their affected part is, and to differentiate how the affected part is being healed. Both the Kiryo practitioner and the Kiryo receiver can follow the healing status of the affected part.

In particular, when we heal internal injuries, the Kiryo practitioner can use their palms to differentiate how and when the Kiryo recipient's pain is removed. The Kiryo practitioner uses their hand feedback sensation to differentiate when the affected part has been healed. This ability to perceive and differentiate also never goes away once it has been obtained.

Ki energy and perceptive and differentiative ability are a pair. They are two sides of the same coin, and they work together mutually to realize healing. In Kiryo, this healing sensation is called the Kiryo sensation. And the sensation that enables us to perceive and differentiate the healing state of affected parts is called the wave sensation (wave perception sensation). In addition, because Kiryo recipients feel that their pain is gone once they have been healed, we refer to their sensation as the healed sensation (naturally healed sensation).

The Nature of Perception & Differentiation

Awakening of the twin sensory nerves (the Kiryo Nerve and the Wave Perception Nerve) allows for mastery of perceptive and differentiative ability, which then allows us to confirm that Ki is existence itself.

In order to protect themselves and keep themselves alive, animals have their wave perception nerves active throughout their body. Humans also have the wave perception nerve throughout their body, but because the humans of today do not need to use it, it remains dormant. We can, however, use exercise (Kiryo mastery) to easily awaken it.

Animals perceive and differentiate with their whole body, but humans have only their sensitive palms. This is the source of the hand feedback sensation. The hand feedback sensation allows us to perceive and differentiate various sorts of waves. We live amongst countless waves. Every object has its own wave.

As explained previously, we can use plants, jewels, and paintings to practice perceptive and differentiative exercise.

One Kiryo practitioner tried exchanging Ki with each tree he would pass by while taking walks in parks or forests. At first, it took him quite a while to perceive the waves of the trees around him, but he eventually became able to perceive waves from each individual tree. The waves of cedar and pine, and ash and elm each had their own hardness or softness, and he learned to differentiate between these using his palms.

I used jewels for this exercise: amethyst, rose quartz, white quartz, agate, lapis lazuli, sunstone, and diamond. The waves of gems are strong, and I think they are quite easy to differentiate between using the hand feedback sensation. When differentiating between rose quartz and amethyst, the waves of the rose quartz feel ticklish and soft, while those of amethyst feel prickly and hard. By the way, the waves of river pebbles and the like are very weak.

One day, after a practice session at a convention for experienced Kiryo practitioners, we all went to an art museum. There were many paintings on display, and we were all surprised that we could perceive strong waves emanating from each. While we took in the works of the famous painters that created the pieces before us, we used our palms to differentiate the various energies coming from each painting. It was great fun.

I do not know why each painting emanates different waves. It may be that the strong passions of their painters remain in these works as residual awareness energy.

Collective Energy and Relaxation Spaces

Collective energy refers to energy created when the energies of individuals collect, amplify, and unify. Relaxation spaces are created after repeatedly collecting and restoring individual energies.

As described in Chapter 1, "Ki Exchanges with Animals," the experiences of more than 300 sheep falling down and staying still, or of more than 200 buffalos in Kenya fell down, truly prove the existence of collective energy. Through this collective energy, a relaxation space—that is, a healing space—was brought forth.

When I began to send Ki to those animals, like the sheep and the buffalo, the Ki exchange between us also began. The Ki chain reaction began to occur between these sheep and buffalo, their individual energies were heightened, collected, amplified, and unified, and they became a single strong collective energy. This strong energy created a relaxation space—a healing space—in which these animals could relax. I guess you could call me the person that sparked the formation of such a space.

The same thing happens even when humans are involved. When exercise begins in our classrooms and lessons, each individual participating in the exercise emits Ki, and they all begin to enter into Ki exchanges. The Ki response sensation is activated, and the Ki chain reaction begins to occur. As the exercises continue, each individual's Ki energy heightens, eventually amplifying and unifying to create a strong collective energy. The classroom or lesson then becomes a relaxation space, a healing space.

Discovery of "Thriving Aged Energy"

Some time ago, I was regularly holding Kiryo classes designed for the elderly residents of a particular senior home.[4] On January 21, 2003, I was close to finishing my third class at the facility; there were about thirty students in attendance. We were sitting in a circle and performing heaven-earth unification exchange. In the middle of the exercise, myself and the other Kiryo practitioners present felt in our palms a fierce energy being emitted by the residents of the senior home.

Their average age was no less than 80 years old. Yet their energy was so strong! I was perplexed. In truth, the energy we felt was a collective energy. The energies of all present in the classroom had collected, amplified, and unified to form a single energy. The classroom had become a relaxing space, a healing space. But that energy had a slightly different quality, a unique feel. You could say that it was the sort of fierce energy that strives to protect a life that is growing older. I decided to call it "thriving aged energy."

Myself and the three other Ki practitioners present had felt this thriving aged energy in our hand feedback sensations. We also noticed the existence of a hybrid energy. It was the mixed energy of life energy and affected-part energy. This energy

---

[4] It is common in Japanese culture to refrain from mentioning specific details regarding past events.

felt noisy and murky. The less noisy and murky this energy became, the more the illnesses of those present had subsided.

Six months later, there was no noise left in the energy of this class, and many residents showed improvement in the symptoms of their illnesses, among which were cardiac failure, cardiac infarction, or myopia. To our surprise, the thriving aged energy had become, through exercise, a rejuvenated, youthful energy. I saw this change in the behavior of the residents that participated in the classes; they became quicker and more light-footed, and seemed more alive. Some of their memories even improved.

The discovery of "thriving aged energy" through the hand feedback sensation was an important one for the sensory world. Further, the discovery that this energy could, through exercise (Kiryo mastery), be changed into rejuvenated, youthful energy was also very important. People with chronic illnesses could, without their own realization, cure what ailed them through natural healing. I was delightfully surprised to hear that many were healed, and I humbly received their thanks. Finally, while healing had become an ordinary occurrence at the academy, these discoveries at the nursing home made me notice again the wonderful effects of Kiryo mastery (exercise).

Preventative and Arrestive Action

I hope I have made it clear that the configurations of Kiryo mastery exercise (both alone and with others) allow one to master both Ki energy and perceptive and differentiative ability. These exercises enable us to draw out and heighten our inner healing power—that is, the natural healing power. This natural healing power helps shape our body so that it cannot fall ill and helps arrest the progress of the illnesses of those who are already ill. Thus, preventative Kiryo ensures that we do not become sick by stopping illnesses before they occur. Healing which stops illnesses from progressing and worsening is called arrestive action.

Preventative Kiryo

Something I often hear from people who suffer from severe illnesses is that "health is most important." A healthy person suddenly attacked by illness and forced to bear intolerable pain knows just how precious health is. Humans have conquered many intractable illnesses through intelligence and wisdom, but that is nowhere near enough.

Techniques are being developed at the cutting edge of medicine, and regenerative treatments made possible by biotechnology are also becoming more and more well-known, but amidst this new landscape, I believe it may also be valuable to return once again to the origin of healing itself.

Kiryo is that origin of healing. It can draw out and heighten our inner healing powers and stop illnesses before they occur.

Once, a patient with cerebral infarctions came to see me. His CT scan apparently indicated that infarctions were dotted all over his cerebrum. His symptoms were a slightly heavy head and mild difficulty speaking. I sent Ki into and around his head, about four or five times. After being retested, he found that he no longer had any infarctions, and his headache was gone. His body even felt light and free.

How was this man healed?

One of the most wonderful aspects of Kiryo is its power to, by stimulating the nerves, improve blood flow without touching the body. As mentioned earlier, an easily seen proof of the power of Ki is as follows: if one holds their palm over the outstretched palm of their partner and waves it, their partner's hand will turn red and white spots will appear. This phenomenon caused by blood collecting in the palm.

The nerves are arranged in such a way that they increase blood flow when stimulated. This is why I have my patients lie down, so I can hold my hand flat above their head and wave it side to side. Since the brain is also a nerve, it is directly stimulated by my Ki, and draws blood into itself. In Kiryo, we consider the blood vessels to act similarly to muscles. The blood vessels inside the brain become soft and supple, and blood is sent to every part of the brain.

Even the parts with brain infarctions get softer, and blood flow through them becomes proper. Good blood flow means nutrients and oxygen are being sufficiently sent to the brain, and dying, necrotized brain cells are revived and vitalized.

When it is properly receiving nutrients and oxygen, the brain is vitalized, and it sends strong brainstem orders to the autonomic nerves, causing them to also become vitalized. Then, it causes smooth blood circulation that prevents the reoccurrence of brain infarctions.

If I were to draw attention to just one thing, it would be this: even though one may be healthy now, it is in their best interest to ensure that they will not fall ill at some point in the future. One can prevent against brain infarct and hemorrhage, too. In Kiryo, it is easy prevent illnesses before they even occur.

Preventative Kiryo awakens the twin sensory nerves and makes active use of the principle of neurotransmissive flux. This principle carries out muscular adjustment, blood flow adjustment, immune adjustment, hormonal adjustment, and psychological adjustment, among other things, making both our body and mind healthy so that we do not fall ill. Mastery of Ki is mastery of this inner healing power which is the natural healing power. In the modern era, where we must protect our health ourselves, preventative Kiryo has become indispensable.

Arrestive Action

When the body is in a state of poor circulation (due to chronic illness, etc.), awakening the twin sensory nerves and converting the body back to a state of proper circulation stops illnesses from progressing. This is known as arrestive action.

People who suffer from chronic illness are in a state of poor circulation. Their whole body's muscles (including their organs) are stiff, and their blood circulation is not good. Normally, when something bad happens, our bodies stiffen, and when something good happen, they relax. Stressors cause the mind and body to stiffen, and blood circulation worsens. When blood circulation worsens, less than enough blood is delivered to the brain, and it begins to lack nutrients and oxygen.

In particular, the homeostatic function of the brainstem lessens. With its functions degraded, the brainstem can only send weak orders to the autonomic nerves. When the autonomic nerves receive these weak orders, their function weakens as well, worsening circulation. Illnesses therefore become hard to heal.

Awakening the twin sensory nerves arrests this vicious cycle of poor circulation.

Most people who attend my school suffer from some kind of illness or are otherwise concerned about their health. After beginning our mastery courses and attending our classes, students notice that their old illnesses have all but vanished. Practicing the configurations of Kiryo mastery exercise caused their illnesses to disappear.

These exercises are nothing but practices for mutually awakening the twin sensory nerves. When the twin sensory nerves are awakened, the principle of neurotransmissive flux is activated, arresting the progress of the students' illnesses, and putting them on the path to recovery. The vicious cycle of poor circulation is stopped, and the students are switched to good and proper circulation. And as these students' mastery of Ki energy increases, their illnesses are naturally healed. The awakening of the twin sensory nerves is the same as arrestive action.

List of Illnesses Healed Through Kiryo Mastery

Which illnesses are the Kiryo mastery exercises effective against?

When I say exercise, I refer to the mutual awakening of the twin sensory nerves through neurotransmissive exchange. When the twin sensory nerves are awakened, the principle of neurotransmissive flux is activated. Neurotransmissive flux carries out muscular adjustment, blood flow adjustment, hormonal adjustment, immune adjustment, and psychological adjustment, among others.

The principle of neurotransmissive flux draws out and heightens inner healing power. It is a natural healing power that arrests the progress of illness and heals us.

Below are the illnesses which the exercises of the mastery courses at the Academy, Kiryo classes, and single-person exchange have been able to naturally heal or manifest the effects of such healing upon.

Headache, migraine, neuropathy, auditory hallucinations, hypertension, hypotension, chronic rhinitis, allergic rhinitis, eye pain, eye fatigue, eye itchiness, dry eye, watery eyes, bronchitis, allergic symptoms, tonsillitis, atopic dermatitis, stress, depression, Meniere's disease, autonomic dysfunction, general malaise, hormonal imbalance, stiff shoulder, frozen shoulder, whiplash syndrome, tendonitis, lumbar pain, slipped disc, arm numbness, bruises, arm pain, knee arthritis, trigger finger, myalgia, muscular contusion, Achilles tendonitis, lacerations, burns, amenorrhea, menstrual irregularity, menstrual pain, uterine myoma, ovarian cyst, chest tightness, thrombosis, myocardial arrhythmia, angina pectoris, myocardial infarction, heart failure, atrial fibrillation, apnea syndrome, stomach pain, anorexia, gastric ulcer, gastroptosis, gastritis, enteritis, duodenal ulcer, diarrhea, constipation, cystitis, nephritis, chronic fatigue, tinnitus, diabetes, complications from diabetes, liver disease, cancer, nervous disorders, spinal correction, sensitivity to cold, anemia, sports injuries, other illnesses of uncertain origin accompanied by pain.

Health Promotion Act

A time in which Kiryo can address the aims of the Health Promotion Act has come.

The health promotion law was promulgated in Japan on August 2, 2002. Please look at Articles 1 (Objective) and 2 (The Duty of the People) below.

Health Promotion Act

(Objective)

Article 1

This law seeks to, in accordance with the rapid progression of societal aging and the changing nature of illness and disease in our country, and in light of the significantly growing importance of the health of the people, through the establishment of basic facts with regards to the implementation of a comprehensive promotion of popular health and the laying out of measures to target the health promotion of the populace, including, but not limited to, nutritional reform, aim for the improvement of national health.

(The Duty of the People)

Article 2

The people must deepen their understanding of and interest in the importance of healthy habits, and, throughout their lives, both be aware of the state of their health and strive towards its improvement.

This is a law created to address the lifestyle diseases that will befall the aging society of Japan. This country is approaching uncharted, unprecedented levels of aging.

There are fewer and fewer children. We have entered an age where the few young must take care of the many old. The labor and economic cost of caring for the ill will have to be shouldered by the young. Our medical insurance system may no longer even be able to function properly.

Under these circumstances, it is important for each one of us to deepen our understanding of and interest in illness (especially lifestyle diseases), and, throughout our lives, both be aware of the state of our health, manage it appropriately, and strive towards its promotion.

In the aging society towards which Japan is heading, there will surely be many ill people. And in such a society, Kiryo mastery (exercise) ought to become a great tool.

Chapter 4: Kiryo Technique

The Makeup of the Human Body from the Perspective of Kiryo

Considering the Makeup of the Human Body

Kiryo is a holistic component treatment method, and is performed in accordance with this idea.

Holistic refers to the fact that the entire body is taken to be the target of healing. Kiryo improves the health of the entire body as a whole.

Component refers to the affected parts of the body. In the event that the Kiryo recipient is suffering from multiple ailments, all of these affected parts are holistically treated at once via Kiryo. They are healed in order of least to most difficult to heal.

Kiryo divides the human body into four large sections as can be seen in the table on the opposing page (refer to Table 6).

The four sections consist of: the skeleton, the muscles, fluids, and the nerves. In Kiryo, the makeup of the human body is referred to as the physiological framework. The nerves are what control this physiological framework.

Via the vitalization of the source of life itself, the brainstem, the twin sensory nerves, and the principle of neurotransmissive flux are activated, and the function of the physiological framework is improved. Strengthening the physiological framework allows one to beat illness.

Table 6: The Makeup of the Human Body in Kiryo

Nerves	Peripheral Nervous System	Motor Nerves			
		Sensory Nerves	Twin Sensory Nerves		
			Five Senses Nerves		
		Autonomic Nerves	Parasympathetic Nerves		
			Sympathetic Nerves		
	Central Nervous System	Spinal Cord	Nervous Junction		
		Brain Tissue	Brainstem		
			Cerebellum		
			Cerebrum		
Fluids	Bodily Fluids	Other Fluids			
		Lymphatic Fluid			
		Hormones	Each Type of Hormone		
		Blood	Blood Plasma		
			Blood Cells	Platelets	
				White Blood Cells	
				Red Blood Cells	
Muscles	Other Muscles				
	Visceral Muscles	Various Internal Organs	Within the Thoracic and Abdominal Cavities		
	Skeletal Muscles	Attached to the Skeleton	Movable Muscle		

Skeleton	Skeletal Tissue	Support of the Body	Facilitation of Movement Protection of Organs

The Spinal and Visceral Muscles are Two Sides of the Same Coin

Generally, I doubt people would believe the fact that the spinal and visceral muscles are two sides of the same coin. I too was unaware of this fact, but eventually realized it after performing Kiryo on many different patients. One patient was suffering from severe pain due to stomach problems. No matter where he went, his stomach refused to heal, so he finally made his way to me.

I asked him to lay face-down, and as he did so, I noticed that part of his back appeared to be raised. It was exactly near his stomach, on both sides of his spine. Upon sending Ki into this raised part and lightly attempting to relax it with my fingers, the raised portion lowered, and became much softer.

After finishing the Kiryo session, I asked the patient how his stomach felt, and he said that the nausea in his stomach had subsided, and that his back felt much better as well. Apparently, his stomach never again troubled him.

Following this incident, I thought for a long time why exactly the disappearance of the raised bump behind this patient's stomach led to the improvement of the condition of his stomach. Additionally, I felt that there may be some secret in the spinal muscles, and that warping of the spinal cord leads to various types of illness. From then on, I focused on correcting the warping of the spine during Kiryo, and by doing so I achieved respectable results. However, it became apparent to me that there were many people that lacked any noticeable warping of the spine and yet still were ill.

Then, one day, while analyzing past symptoms of previous patients, I came upon a certain pattern. Namely, I realized that rather than warping of the spinal bones, compression of the nerves emanating from the spinal cord was causing illness.

Why, then, does compression of the spinal cord nerves occur?

Impartial stiffening of the spinal muscles. Specifically, stiffening of the spinal muscles that are on the side of the organs compresses the spinal cord nerves. When the spinal cord nerves are compressed, orders from the brainstem to the internal organs are transmitted in a weakened form, and the activity of the internal organs is thereby itself weakened. As a result, when the spinal muscles right behind an organ begin to hurt or swell outwards, it must be case that the organ itself is in some sort of abnormal state.

Kiryo possesses the ability to make muscles softer. It will soften impartially stiffened, swollen muscles, making them flat once again and thereby lessening one's pain. Consequently, the visceral-side spinal muscles will become softer, eliminating compression of the spinal cord nerves, allowing for the unaltered transmission of the orders of the brainstem, leading to proper, unimpeded functioning of the organs.

In Kiryo, the spinal cord is referred to as the nervous junction. The spinal cord is like a junction, a road where the brain and peripheral nerves meet. As long as there is no compression of the spinal cord nerves, transmission between the brain and peripheral nerves remains smooth, and the function of the various organs remains good, and illness can be beaten.

Kiryo can train the viscera (and visceral muscles) via the twin sensory nerves and the principle of neurotransmissive flux. The more they are trained, the softer the visceral muscles become. When practicing Kiryo or doing Kiryo exercise, people may notice their stomach rumbling. This is nothing but the softening of all the visceral muscles.

The Five Principles of Skeletal Muscle Kiryo Technique

Skeletal (orthopedic) healing is the specialty of Kiryo. Over many years and through much practice, I have come to realize that Kiryo of the skeletal muscles can be accomplished through an exceedingly easy method that still produces extraordinary results. This method wonderfully soothes the pain caused by swelling of the skeletal muscles.

(1) Send Ki into the affected area when the muscles are in their natural (relaxed) state.
(2) Send Ki into the affected area when the muscles are in an elongated state.
(3) Send Ki into the affected area when the muscles are in a contracted state.
(4) Ki into the affected area when the muscles when they are on a bias (in a diagonal) state.
(5) If, by confirmation from the patient, there is pain in the affected area, send Ki into the area in the orientation that causes the pain.

If the above principles numbered (1) to (5) are followed in that order, save for symptoms of exceptional illnesses, anyone trained in the principles of Kiryo technique can easily quell their pain.

For example, let me explain the Kiryo method in the context of tenosynovitis of the wrist.

(1) Send Ki from approximately four inches above the wrist as it is placed on a table.
(2) Send Ki into the wrist when it is bent and the muscles are elongated.

(3) Send Ki into the wrist when it is bent the other direction and the same muscles are now contracted.

(4) Send Ki into the wrist when it is on a bias (twisted into a diagonal orientation).

(5) Ask the patient to move his/her wrist, and if it still hurts, send Ki into it in the orientation in which it hurts.

Muscular Adjustment and Blood Flow Adjustment

Muscular adjustment, and thereby blood flow adjustment, will always occur in the patient as he or she receives Kiryo. This fact was made clear to me over many years of frequently practicing Kiryo. This applies to Kiryo mastery (exercise) as well, but when performing Kiryo, both the performer and the recipient experience muscular adjustment, and thereby blood flow adjustment and blood flow improvement. This is because the physiological framework (the principle of neurotransmissive flux) makes it so.

By the power of the heart alone, blood cannot be sent to every corner of the body. It is impossible for blood to reach every corner of our bodies without the assistance of the skeletal and visceral muscles. The thigh and calf muscles are particularly good at pumping blood strongly. They are sometimes even called the second heart.

The occurrence that muscular adjustment and blood flow adjustment begin the moment one directs their awareness towards Ki is a wonderful property of the human body that never fails to amaze me.

Basics of Kiryo Technique

Forms of Basic Kiryo Technique

Kiryo technique is quite easy, and their Kiryo effects are strong. They heal the Kiryo practitioners that perform them as well. Why is this so? Earlier, I explained the nature of the physiological framework (the principle of neurotransmissive flux). However, there is one more very important concept to consider. It is to perform Kiryo while feeling as you are: without using the cerebrum or motor nerves, one switches to the sensory world, allow themselves to become a medium for the natural energy known as Ki, and send Ki.

The more one uses their brain and motor nerves, the more tired they get. When one exhausts them, they become overworked, and may even fall ill as a result. Kiryo simply involves becoming medium of natural energy; we do not use our brain or motor nerves, and we do not, therefore, get tired. When I was in Kenya, racing in that jeep across the prairie, making animals fall down left and right, I never felt fatigued or tired.

When I say "tired," I mean that the act of using Ki will not tire us. We do get a bit more tired when performing Kiryo on humans. As living, breathing humans, we tire from any sort of labor. Since Kiryo involves entering one's natural state and becoming a medium of natural energy, its healing power is strong. Kiryo practitioners should not attempt to actively heal their patients with their own Ki energy; they will only tire themselves out.

At this point, I would like to explain the forms of basic Kiryo technique. I will number them to indicate the order in which these forms should be practiced.

1. Check the pulse; 2. Head; 3. Heart; 4. Lower abdomen; 5. Sole; 6. Affected part; 7. Check the pulse again.

*Before moving forward, let me explain once more the Kiryo term "hand-waving."

"Hand-waving" refers to the act of holding one's hand four inches away from the affected part of the Kiryo recipient, with the palm facing it, and waving the hand back and forth laterally. Hand-waving came to me naturally while I was practicing Kiryo, and I use it all the time now. This is because sending Ki into the affected part while waving the hand makes it easier to catch its recovery reaction through the hand feedback sensation. Hand-waving heals the affected part and also allows one to feel and distinguish its Ki at the same time: it is a very useful tool.

Generally speaking, Kiryo is performed with the recipient lying on his or her back, face-up. This position allows both the recipient and the Ki practitioner to assume natural, convenient positions.

1. Check the pulse.

Before starting Kiryo, the practitioner must always check the pulse of the recipient at the wrist. It may be a good idea for the recipient to check their own pulse, too. This allows us to notice changes in the pulse after treatment has finished.

2. Head

Send Ki with hand-waving to the following parts of the head in the order they are listed: crown, forehead and both sides of the head. The recipient's body will react immediately to the Ki being sent into their head, and will begin drawing blood to the brain. The circulation of blood in the brain will improve. Further, hand-waving allows us to achieve a massage-like effect on the brain without touching it. Regenerative metabolism will take place, and the brain will become fresh and clean. The brainstem will be vitalized as it receives more nutrients and oxygen, and the principle of neurotransmissive flux will activate. This will help prevent cerebral hemorrhage, stroke or dementia.

3. Heart

The heart is a very important organ; it pumps blood to the whole body. Kiryo has the ability to massage organs without touching them; we will therefore perform hand-waving while sending Ki to the heart in order to massage it. Doing so will soften the muscles of the heart, improve blood flow through the coronary arteries, and pump blood harder to the body parts. This prevents heart attack and myocardial infarction.

4. Lower Abdomen

By "lower abdomen," I mean the part of the stomach below the belly button. It is said that tightening the lower abdomen allows one to obtain health and courage. When we use hand-waving to send Ki to this area, that Ki will be distributed throughout the body.

5. Sole

Sole Kiryo was a big discovery for the practice of Kiryo. The soles have the ability to emit very strong Ki. Kiryo practitioners should send Ki with either of their soles to both of the soles of their recipients. We will send strong Ki to the capillaries, the peripheral nerves, and the central nerves. Doing this will carry out further muscular adjustment and blood adjustment, and improve the recipient's health level.

6. Affected Part

The affected part of a patient can be anything from the entire body to some tiny nook or cranny; there are many possibilities. By performing Kiryo to the head, heart, lower abdomen and soles, the affected area should mostly be healed. Now, when we finally perform Kiryo directly to the affected area, its healing is complete.

7. Check the Pulse Again

When Kiryo is finished, check the pulse again. Let the recipient check it themselves as well.

As explained before, there should be five changes noticeable in the pulse. These changes are described by the following five words: composed, soft, steady, strong, and plump. These five changes in the pulse signify that the functions of the sympathetic nervous system and parasympathetic nervous system and their balance has improved, and that the autonomic nerves have been vitalized.

The changes in pulse before and after the Kiryo are the proof that Kiryo can heal many diseases and sometimes even cause miraculous recovery and restoration of the health of our bodies.

Bare Hand/Foot Kiryo

Kiryo should be performed with your Ki-dominant hand. As you practice and master Kiryo, you will notice that either your left or right hand will become your Ki-dominant hand. Use this Ki-dominant hand when performing Kiryo on a recipient. Using both hands does not produce any change in the effects of Kiryo. It only makes your arms and shoulders tired during long Kiryo treatments. Kiryo should not be a burden to the Kiryo practitioner.

Similarly, while using one's foot to perform Kiryo, they use just one foot. However, unlike with the hands, we switch between our feet so that each foot is used equally. Initially, I only used my right foot, but, as time passed, I taught myself to use my left foot as well, depending on the part of the body I was treating.

Standards of Perception & Differentiation

Perception / Differentiation of Internal Bodily Information

Bodily information is information about the changing of states inside the body of a human being.

Human bodies are constantly changing in order to continue living. Of course, illnesses and injuries cause change, but so do sadness, anger, happiness, and joy. Nervousness and stress can also effect change.

A while back, there was a man who was receiving Kiryo treatment from me on a regular basis for his ailing kidney. His kidney had almost fully recovered, and his bodily information was positive.

One day, I was preparing to perform Kiryo on him, and I had him lie down face up. As I put my palm near the crown of his head, I felt a strong, sharp hand-feedback unlike any I had felt before. I asked him if something had happened, and he said he had had an argument with someone just before the treatment and he was still angry.

His anger caused changes to his body that became sharp waves that entered my palm. I perceived and differentiated those waves of anger with the hand-feedback sensation. That man said, "How did you know?" in surprise when I noticed his anger.

I described in the section titled "The Nature of Perception & Differentiation" that through the hand feedback sensation we can perceive and differentiate various sorts of waves. In order to better understand how use this power to heal illness and injury, I will now explain that topic in further detail (refer to Table 7).

Table 7 is a chart of the standards of perception and differentiation that was drawn up after collecting information about my own hand feedback sensations through long years of Kiryo practice as well as the hand feedback sensations of my students and other Kiryo practitioners. The foot feedback sensation also conforms to the standards listed in this table. While it is far weaker than the hand feedback sensation, the foot feedback sensation can be used to perform approximate perception and differentiation.

The hand-feedback sensation can be separated into two categories: "pain sensations" and "pain-like sensations." "Pain sensations" are hand feedback sensations that are very clearly hurtful, and "pain-like sensations" are hand feedback sensations that are not clearly hurtful. There seems to be a feeling that falls in between these categories as well. Because hand feedback sensations vary greatly from person to person, the most important thing is to make sure you can perceive and differentiate. The nature of the sensation itself is not as crucial.

Table 7: Standards of Perception and Differentiation

Hand Feedback Sensation			
Pain Sensations and Pain-Like Sensations			
1	2	3	4
Strength and weakness	Type	Hardness and softness Tightness and looseness	Clearness and murkiness

(1) The Strength and Weakness of the Pain or Pain-like Sensation

When performing Kiryo on illnesses and injuries, we place our awareness in our palms. As you send Ki to the affected part while performing hand-waving, the affected part is stimulated, and undergoes a recovery reaction as it tries to heal itself.

Kiryo practitioners perceive the waves emitted by recovery reaction in their palms. The stronger the reaction is, the stronger the waves it emits. As the affected part recovers and is healed, the recovery reaction waves emitted by it weaken, and that weakening is also perceived by the Kiryo practitioner.

This is how the practitioner perceives the strength or weakness of the waves of the recovery reaction. Identifying the strength or weakness of the wave through the hand feedback sensation, means one has differentiated it. When you differentiate that the wave has weakened, you will know that the pain in the affected area has been alleviated, and that it has been healed. The Kiryo recipient will of course also notice that the pain in their affected has lessened, and thereby know that it has been healed.

(2) The Type of the Pain or Pain-Like Sensation

When I ask first-time Kiryo practitioners how their hand feedback feels, many of them struggle to come up with a clear answer, and usually end up saying that it feels warm. They tend to mistakenly believe that this warmth is body heat, and not the warmth of Ki itself.

I have told you many stories of just how difficult it is to grasp and express the myriad natures of the hand feedback sensation. However, we have the rich emotive capacity of language at our disposal. Each one of us can, in our own words, describe the type of hand feedback sensation we feel in our palms. The sensations described by these words allow us to perceive and differentiate the waves being emitted by the affected parts of our recipients.

Once one has performed Kiryo on many different people, they can use the type of affected part and the strength of its recovery reaction to master many different types of sensations. The more one practices, the better their perceptive and differentiative ability becomes. Kiryo is rooted in practice and experience.

(3) The Hardness or Softness and Tightness or Looseness of the Pain or Pain-Like Sensation

When we consider the hardness, softness, tightness, and looseness of the sensation, we should know that hardness is the same as tightness, and softness is the same as looseness. It is just that the sensory perception of these qualities differs from person to person. I will use hardness and softness in my explanations here.

Waves have hardness and softness to them. I played a game with my Academy students where we lined up several different gems and compared the waves of each. Gems are sometimes called power stones because they emit strong waves. When one places several gems in a row and perform hand-waving four inches away from them, they can clearly identify the differences in the waves coming from each of them. Anyone can tell you that the wave of this stone "feels strong," or "feels weak." While there are some differences from person to person, when someone perceives strong waves, their palm stiffens and contracts. And when perceiving very strong waves, the hand forms a fist.

Back in Kenya, the moment I began conducting Ki exchange with a rhino, I perceived its fierce and hard feedback waves, and my hand immediately became a fist.

It is common for us to differentiate between hardness and softness by taking note of stiffness in the hand and the shape of the hand itself. This can be quite useful when perceiving and differentiating the recovery reactions of illnesses and injuries. During Kiryo, when the waves transition from a hard state to a soft state, you can say with certainty that the affected part is halfway through being recovered and restored. And in the case of injuries, the recipient will be able to feel that their pain has lessened by more than half.

(4) Clearness and Murkiness of the Pain or Pain-Like Sensation

A great deal of Kiryo practice and a strong perceptive and differentiative ability are needed to perceive and differentiate clearness and murkiness. With (1) strength and weakness, (2) type, and (3) hardness and softness, we are quite capable of perceiving and differentiating the degree of recovery of an illness or injury during treatment. Adding clearness and murkiness to the mix simply makes it that much easier to perceive and differentiate the degree of recovery.

Clearness indicates a state of health. This is the sensation felt by the Kiryo practitioner during treatment when their recipient becomes healthy. These waves are peaceful, composed, and steady. Only normal, proper biological functions produce this clear feeling. If one perceives and differentiates this clear feeling, they can know that whatever illness or injury was present has been healed.

On the other hand, murkiness indicates an unhealthy state, where one suffers the pain of illness and injury. This is the disordered, chaotic sensation felt by the Kiryo practitioner during treatment. It indicates that the recipient's body, having received Ki, is fighting against its injury or illness, trying to heal itself. It is a type of recovery reaction.

Perceiving this murkiness allows one to differentiate the state of an illness or injury. As the recipient recovers their health, this murkiness will be gone. Then the clearness would come, and you can perceive and differentiate that the wound or sickness is healed.

Because the space in which these practices exist is truly a sensory world, I have struggled considerably in verbalizing them. In this sensory world, each person has their own capabilities. While there may be differences from person to person in the degree to which one can apply these standards of perception and differentiation to themselves, as we level up our perceptive and differentiative ability, we will become better able to make use of them.

Kiryo Results

The future will be an age of preventative Kiryo made possible by Kiryo mastery. Otherwise, the people will be unable to contribute productively to the aging society.

One must not forget how wonderful Kiryo effects brought about by its implementation can be. The steadily accumulated achievements of Kiryo enabled the epochal discovery of Kiryo mastery exercise. One might claim that the exercises were "developed" or "formulated" after much thought, but the truth is that the exercise configurations (of Kiryo mastery) came into being quite naturally and spontaneously. In fact, the implementation of Kiryo itself was carried out naturally and spontaneously, in a state of "feeling as you are."

The implementation of Kiryo was the beginning of many discoveries. Without the wonderful effects of Kiryo, there would have been no discovery of the sensory world and the twin sensory nerves that all of us possess. I daresay none of us would have noticed these things at all.

Fundamental Tenets of Kiryo

Kiryo is Naturalness

When doing or receiving Kiryo, it is fundamental that one rid oneself of all thought, and simply be and feel as they are.

Kiryo is Becoming a Medium for Natural Energy

Becoming a medium for the natural energy known as Ki is fundamental to Kiryo. One should not think of this as solo healing, without any assistance.

Kiryo is Not Absolute

Kiryo is not an absolute solution, but its effects are significant and wonderful.

Kiryo is Surrendering to the Physiological Framework

When performing Kiryo, one should leave the heavy lifting to the Kiryo recipient's physiological framework. By doing so, the principle of neurotransmissive flux is activated in the Kiryo recipient, Kiryo effects are manifested, and he or she is healed.

Kiryo Heals the Practitioner Too

When it comes to Kiryo, as a Kiryo practitioner performs Kiryo, he or she also becomes healthy. When performing Kiryo on a Kiryo recipient, neurotransmissive exchange occurs, and the principle of neurotransmissive flux activates in the body of the

Kiryo practitioner as well, leading to the manifestation of Kiryo effects and health itself.

Let us all heal as many as we can, give them the chance to be happy, and receive their gratitude. In doing so, we will become healthy ourselves. In this regard, Kiryo is truly the ideal healing method.

Kiryo Case List

The illnesses I will list here are those that I and the other Kiryo practitioners and academy students have performed Kiryo upon, and managed to manifest Kiryo effects in.

- Headache, Migraine, Psychosomatic Illness, Nervous Disorders, Depression, Panic Disorder, Depersonalization, Auditory Hallucination, Autonomic Dysfunctional Disorder, Cerebral Infarct, Cerebral Hemorrhage, Subarachnoid Hemorrhage, Parkinson's Disease, Trigeminal Neuralgia, Facial Neuralgia, Dementia, Brain Tumor, Cerebral Aneurysm
- Shoulder Stiffness, Frozen Shoulder, Whiplash Injury, Tenosynovitis, Lower Back Pain, Slipped Disk, Sciatica, Arm Nmbness, Bruises, Arm Pain, Knee Arthritis, Muscular Contusion, Achilles Tendonitis, Laceration, Burns, Corns
- Tracheitis, Bronchitis, Bronchial Asthma, Bronchiectasis, Emphysema, Hyperventilation Syndrome, Sleep Apnea Syndrome, Tonsillitis
- Esophagitis, Esophageal Achalasia, Esophageal Aneurysm, Gastritis, Gastroptosis, Gastric Ulcer, Duodenum, Gastric Cancer, Gastric Polyp, Gastric Distension, Acute Enteritis, Irritable Bowel Syndrome, Constipation, Ulcerative Colitis, Colonic Polyp, Intestinal Obstruction, Gastralgia, Anorexia, Diarrhea, Hepatitis, Hepatic Cirrhosis, Hepatic Steatosis,

Alcoholic Liver Disease, Cholelithiasis, Hemorrhoids, Oral Ulcers

- Cardiac Infarct, Angina Pectoris, Myocarditis, Arrhythmia, Arteriosclerosis, High Blood Pressure, Atrial Fibrillation, Cardiac Hypertrophy, Diastolic Heart Disease, Low Blood Pressure, Arterial Aneurysm, Venous Aneurysm, Sensitivity to Cold, Blood Circulation Disorder, Raynaud's Syndrome, Nephritis, Renal Failure, Renal Calculus, Urethral Calculus, Cystitis, Pollakiuria, Anemia, Urethra, Prostatic Hyperplasia
- Diabetes, Complications due to Diabetes, Hyperthyroidism, Hypothyroidism, Hormonal Imbalance
- Eye Disease, Eye Strain, Eye Itch, Dry Eye, Watery Eye, Keratoconus, Cataract, Glaucoma, Conjunctivitis
- Tinnitus, Otitis Media, Otitis Externa, Meniere's Disease, Rhinitis, Allergic Rhinitis, Tonsillitis,
- Infertility, Uterine Myoma, Ovarian Cyst, Symptoms of Pregnancy, Amenorrhea, Menstrual Irregularity, Menstrual Pain, Breast Cancer
- Atopic Dermatitis, Rheumatism, Spinal Correction, Sports Injury
- Other Illnesses of Uncertain Origin Accompanied by Pain

Arrestive Action and Preventative Kiryo (Recap)

In Chapter 3, "Kiryo Mastery," I discussed in detail preventative Kiryo and arrestive action. Here, I would like to discuss some important things to keep in mind when engaging in Kiryo.

In the many years I have been doing Kiryo, it has been my experience that most all Kiryo patients come seeking complete healing. One day, while speaking to a Kiryo patient of mine, I said rather nonchalantly that, "we should focus on arresting the progress of the illness first." At that moment, that patient's lifeless, hollow eyes sparkled brightly.

The moment I looked at those eyes, I realized just how important the words I had just said were. Right then and there, I came up with the idea of "arrestive action." My patient, cowed by the burden of their depressive feelings, suddenly began to look alive again. The energy that prompts one to continue to live on had welled up once again inside them. Sometime later, I learned that that patient had recovered their health completely. From that day onward, I decided to discuss the idea of "arrestive action" with my patients. These words help lighten the nature of the relationship between the Kiryo practitioner and Kiryo patient.

Ki energy, before making one completely well, works first to arrest the progress of one's illnesses. Thus, some of the most important words in Kiryo practice are "arrestive action."

Preventative Kiryo is Kiryo that ensures, through the activation of the principle of neurotransmissive flux, that even though one may not be currently afflicted with an illness, one's body will remain healthy.

Afterword

Here, I would like to tell you about my father, in the hope that the story of his relationship with Kiryo may beof some use to you.

My father spent his youth in the war, and afterwards, took up a living as a joiner craftsman. During the war, he suffered from malaria on the battlefield, but was able to recover from it. At the age of 68, he developed stomach cancer, underwent surgery, and had two-thirds of his stomach removed. By the time he was seventy, it had spread to his lungs. His weight fell to a mere eighty pounds, and was told by doctors that he had little more than three months to live. However, a newly-discovered anti-cancer drug proved to be highly effective on him, and he began to recover. Within half a year, his weight returned to around 120 pounds, and he achieved a frankly miraculous victory over his cancer at last.

Soon after, I experienced my wave perception shock, awoke to the nature of Ki, and developed the ability to heal other's illnesses and injuries. Seeing this, my father decided that he, too, should be able to do whatever his son could, and therefore began to practice Kiryo exercise every day with the palms of his hands. He did what I now call gap-adjustment exchange, ki-kneading, and open-close exchange. Initially, he said he didn't feel any hand feedback sensation at all, but he continued to practice diligently. Eventually, his hand feedback sensation began to emerge, ever so slightly, and he was overjoyed.

After ten months of practice, he began to perform Kiryo on his neighbors and relatives. To his surprise, almost all of them were healed. He had, almost unknowingly, mastered both Ki energy and perceptive/differentiative ability. His achievements were even reported in his local newspaper. He was 75.

From then on, until he passed away at 87—almost 12 years—he was able to assist those suffering from illness and injury, and would often proclaim that he was, "the happiest man on earth!"

All of you who have done me the immense favor of picking up this book, young and old alike, let us perform Kiryo exercise to awaken the twin sensory nerves that lie dormant within us all. And let us all practice preventative Kiryo to ward off future illness, as well.

Those of you lying in hospitals, or those of you suffering even now from illness—you, too, can perform Kiryo exercise. Awaken your twin sensory nerves, recover your health, and reap the benefits of natural healing. Even those of you slowly rehabilitating yourself through therapy, or those of you drained by the demands of nursing a loved one—I believe this can help all of you.

Kiryo is possessed by all, regardless of race, age, or sex. We need only awaken the twin sensory nerves that lie dormant within each of us. After all, is it not the duty of the people to, "throughout their lives, both be aware of the state of their health and strive towards its improvement," that the Health Promotion Act urges for us?

Glossary

Arrestive Action (進行防止) - Preventing a current illness or injury from getting worse. This is one of the natural effects of Kiryo.

Hand Feedback Sensation (手応感覚) - The various different sensations felt in the palm in response to Ki. These are a product of the interaction between Ki and the nervous system. Perceiving and distinguishing these sensations is the task of the perception distinguishing nerve.

Ki Chain Reaction (気応連鎖) - The Ki chain reaction refers to what happens when, after one being receives Ki, the Ki response travels to another being.

Kiryo Nerve (気療神経) – One of the twin sensory nerves. The Kiryo nerve uses the power of Ki to heal and prevent against illness and injury. Just as perceptive/differentiative ability is the task of the wave perception nerve, Ki energy is the task of the Kiryo nerve.

Ki Response Sensation (気応感覚) - A comprehensive term referring to the feedback sensations felt in all parts of the body in response to Ki energy.

Kiryo Wisdom (気療心得) – Another term for the guiding principles of Kiryo, which are as follows: Ki is a natural energy possessed by all beings and things, and Kiryo is becoming a medium for natural energy.

Neurotransmissive Flux Principle (神経伝達還流の原理)
– The interactions that occur between the twin sensory nerves, the brainstem, and the autonomic nerves once the twin sensory nerves have been awakened. The beginning of neurotransmissive flux between these structures allows for the vitalization of the physiological framework of our bodies, and manifestation of the healing effects of Kiryo. See Diagram 3 on page 87.

Perceptive/Differentiative Ability (感知判別能力) – The ability to perceive and differentiate between the various different kinds of waveforms emitted by objects and beings in nature. This ability is heightened through regular, diligent Kiryo practice.

Preventative Kiryo (予防気療) - Preventing future illness or injury. This is one of the natural effects of Kiryo.

Wave Perception Nerve (波動感知神経) – The nerve that gives us our perceptive/differentiative ability. This is one of the twin sensory nerves, and its activity allows us to perceive and differentiate the various different energies present in nature.

Author Timeline - Tadashi Kanzawa

January 1944	Born in Gunma Prefecture.
March 1968	Graduates from the Department of Law at Meiji University.
December 1971	Begins work as a civil servant.
January 1988	Strange things happen to his body. From January to March, brainstem shocks happen a total of six times, all during the middle of the night, while asleep. Because of this, he is awakened to the power of Ki (self-healing power), heals several of his own illnesses, and realizes that this is effective against the illnesses and injuries of others as well. Since then, he has healed tens of thousands of people.
March 1992	Quits his civil service position and goes to Tokyo.
April 1992	Devotes himself to the research and practice of the power of Ki and begins to spread word about the power of Ki.
July 1994	Stays for one month in Avignon, France, to spread word about the power of Ki.
February 1995	Publishes *Kiryo* (Tama Publishers).
May 1996	Publishes *Remote Kiryo* (Tama Publishers)
August 1996	Founds the Kiryo School. Opens the Kyoto branch in February 1997.
November 1997	Appears on TBS Television's "Bizarre Animals!"
June 1998	Appears on Fuji Television's "Miraculous Experiences! Unbelievable!"
August 1998	Opens the Kiryo Academy (renames the "Kiryo School")
July 1999	Opens the Paris branch of the Kiryo Academy.

April 2001	Appears on Asahi Televison's "For Real?! Australia Edition."
October 2001	Appears on Asahi Television's "For Real?! Spain Edition."
December 2001	Appears on Asahi Television's "For Real?! Kenya Edition."
June 2002	Appears on Korea TV's Japan-Korea World Cup Commemorative Special Program.
August 2002	Opens the San Francisco branch of the Kiryo Academy.
October 2002	Appears on Asahi Television's "For Real?! Siberia Edition."
November 2003	Appears on a BBC program (shot in Japan). Scheduled for broadcast in July 2004.
February 2004	Publishes *Healing With Kiryo* (Tama Publishers)

Similar Reads

The Study of Kiryo: Awaken the Symbiotic Healing Power – Tadashi Kanzawa

Enter Mo Pai: The Ancient Training of the Immortals – James Van Gelder

Enter the Infinite – James Van Gelder

Healing With Kiryo
(Health Promotion Through Kiryo)
1/25/2018   First Edition, First Press

Author	Tadashi Kanzawa
Publisher	James Van Gelder
Publishing House	Wheel of Knowledge Publishing

〒Wheel of Knowledge Publishing
http://www.WheelofKnowledge.org
Transfer (Japanese Version): 00130-5-94804

Made in the USA
Columbia, SC
27 January 2018